How To PRAY for Your CHILDREN

by Quin Sherrer

AGLOW®

INTERNATIONAL

P.O. Box 1548
Lynwood, WA 98046-1548
USA

Cover design by Kathy Boice
Cover photo by Jim & Mary Whitmer
Cover calligraphy by Katherine Malmsten

Aglow International is an interdenominational organization of Christian women. Our mission is to lead women to Jesus Christ and provide opportunity for Christian women to grow in their faith and minister to others.

Our publications are used to help women find a personal relationship with Jesus Christ, to enhance growth in their Christian experience, and help them recognized their roles and relationship according to Scripture.

For more information about our organization, please write to Aglow International, P.O. Box 1548, Lynnwood, WA 98046-1548, USA or call (206) 775-7282.

Unless otherwise noted, all scripture quotations in this publication are from the Holy Bible, New International Version. Copyright 1973, 1978, 1984, International Bible Society. Other versions are abbreviated as follows: TAB (The Amplified Bible), KJV (King James Version), TLB (the Living Bible).

ISBN 0-932395-33-4
10 11 12 Printing/Year 96 95

Acknowledgements

We appreciate permission to use portions of material from *Learning How to Pray for Our Children* by Quin Sherrer, published by Agape Ministries, 2600 Park Avenue, Titusville, FL 32780.

Special thanks also to the Rev. Peter Lord, pastor of Park Avenue Baptist Church, Titusville, Florida, who with his wife Johnnie, gave permission to share some of their pains and victories in raising five children; and to all the other parents who were willing to be transparent in sharing their stories.

Table of Contents

Foreword

It was twenty years ago when we realized our number four child had a reading disability. He had completed his first year in school and it was obvious something was wrong. We enrolled him in a Christian school where he repeated first grade. It was a disaster. He was no further along than when he was in kindergarten.

We had him tested. Although he had a high IQ, the tests indicated he had certain learning disabilities which hindered him in reading and writing. We put him under a reading specialist, had him tutored, sent him to clinics, put him in glasses for a year, enrolled him in a class where he spent agonizing hours putting pegs in holes, walking balance beams, and crawling under ropes stretched low to the ground. We even took him to a Kathryn Kuhlman healing service. Nothing seemed to be working. Although he was back in public school, the teachers didn't do much with him but advance him along with the class—even though he could barely read and write.

When he was in the fourth grade, I realized I could not depend on anyone else to help him. It was up to God. And me. My part was to pray. God's part was to heal. Gradually, I came to understand that while God could heal him instantly, He had more in mind. He wanted to teach me how to pray for my son—and He wanted my son to learn how to receive my love and appreciate my prayers. For the next ten years I never missed a night, if I was home, going into his room when he went to bed, sitting on the side of the bed, talking and praying with my son.

The talking was important. I wanted him to know that regardless of the fact he had a problem, his mom and dad—and his brother and sisters—were proud of him. We did not blame him for his problem, nor did we see him as any different than the other children. In our eyes he was simply our son. If he'd had a bad day, I encouraged him. I wanted him to know he was loved and needed and appreciated in our family. I wanted the last thoughts to enter his mind before he went to sleep—the thoughts which would influence his subconscious during the night hours—to be positive thoughts.

But I am convinced that while the parental encouragement kept him well-adjusted socially and drew him into a deep love relationship with the family, it was the prayers which brought the healing.

Two years after he finished high school (thanks to a splendid teacher who took him on as a special project and helped him graduate—even though he was only reading at a fourth grade level), he came to me and said, "Dad, I'll always be a common laborer unless I go to college like the other kids in the family. I want to enter agricultural college and learn to work with animals."

Again, we encouraged him even though all the odds were against him. This time my wife and I had to pray for him in absentia as he struggled, along with his faithful wife, to master textbooks on horticulture, animal anatomy, and farm management by listening to tapes. But he persevered. And God answered our prayers.

When he graduated, he was reading at college level. Today he holds a fine job as a ranch manager, responsible for prize animals worth tens of thousands of dollars each.

Proud of our son? You bet! But far more, Jackie and I are grateful to a loving and faithful God who answers the prayers of parents for children.

Jamie Buckingham
Palm Bay, Florida

Introduction

Christian mothers are hurting for their children today. Mothers are weeping for kids who have run away from home, who are pregnant but not married, who are involved in drugs, sex, or occult activities.

Last year I stayed overnight in the home of a Christian couple whose twenty-eight-year-old son had just quit a good-paying job because his mind was in confusion. Mental illness, a disease once uncommon with the young, is no longer rare; in fact, recent surveys show that over one-half of all mental patients are now in their twenties or younger.

In Texas last month a mother brought her sixteen-year-old daughter to hear me speak at a meeting. The girl confessed to me afterward that she was involved in Satan worship. Another mother at the same meeting asked prayer for her son who had just received a fifteen-year prison sentence for manslaughter.

I have held mothers in my arms while we've wept before the Lord for our children—theirs and mine—so I know how hearts are breaking with hopelessness.

Not long ago when I was depressed over a situation with one of our youngsters, I picked up a book by a well-known Christian author. For the first time she confessed her four-year estrangement from her only daughter. She could write about it now, she said, because their relationship had been restored. The daughter now was happily married to a Christian young man. He met all the qualifications the mother had for ten years prayed that her future son-in-law would have. What hope rose within me.

Mothers, take heart. No matter how hopeless, how impossible your situation, God has the answer. He wants to woo our lost, damaged children back to Himself. To do this, He needs our prayers.

An intercessor must love enough to take another's place. Only a mother or father or grandparent—or God—can understand the depth of parental love.

One

Praying for Our Children

"[Jesus] said to them, 'Let the little children come to me....'And he took the children in his arms, put his hands on them and blessed them'' (Mark 10:14,16).

"How do you do it? How do you have the stamina to keep going out into that surf?" a tourist asked Keith, my college-age son, one muggy summer morning. She had watched him pull the fourth swimmer in distress from the Gulf's riptide.

Keith caught his breath as he lay exhausted on the beach beside his lifeguard station, then squinted through the sun to look her in the eye. "Lady, I know I have someone praying for me almost constantly—my mom."

I'm sorry to admit he couldn't always have said that, because for years I was a crisis pray-er. When my children got sick, I tried to bargain with God, promising Him all sorts of things if He would only honor my prayer. The rest of the time I uttered general "bless us" prayers.

13

Somewhere along the way, I finally realized that if God gave me three children to rear, it was my responsibility—no, my privilege—to come to Him often on their behalf. But I honestly didn't know how. Prayer had to have a deeper dimension than I had experienced. Thus I set out on a prayer pilgrimage of my own—searching the Bible and listening to others pray. Everywhere I went, I asked mothers, "How do you pray for your children?"

In the ensuing dozen years I've discovered some basic "how-tos" which have helped me, and I'm passing them on to you. The following guidelines have proved successful for many parents:

Prayer Helps

1. Be specific. Remember, the blind man told Jesus specifically, "I want to see."

2. Pray Scripture passages aloud. Hearing our own voices speak God's Word excites our faith. The Bible says, *"Faith comes from hearing the message, and the message is heard through the word of Christ" (Rom. 10:17).* Reading Scripture is not some magic formula, but the Bible does provide us with good prayer patterns to follow. Consider Jesus' teachings on *saying:*

"If anyone says to this mountain, 'Go, throw yourself into the sea, and does not doubt in his heart but believes that what he says will happen, it will be done for him" (Mark 11:23.).

As we pray what Scripture says about our children, the power of God's Word drives out anxiety and fear and produces faith in us. A Bible teacher explained it this way: "The things we say are the things we will eventually believe, and the things we believe are things we will eventually receive."

3. Write out your prayers in a notebook, listing the day you asked. Then record when and how the Lord answered. This, too, builds our faith.

After Moses broke the tablets of stone, God rewrote His commandments, thus showing the importance of His written covenant with Israel. Throughout the Bible, prophecies are recorded for us to read so we will understand the ways of God. In Psalm 102:18 we read, *"Let this be written for a future generation, that a people not yet created may praise the Lord."*

God commanded the prophet Habbakuk to record the vision which He had given him so it would be a witness in the end times. When God speaks to us, we may forget what He says, but if we write it down, we and our children and their children after them will have proof of God's covenant relationship with us. They will praise the Lord because of it.

4. Ask God for the things that are on His heart, and pray His prayers for our children.

5. Remember that some prayers will be "waiting prayers." If we pray for our children's future mates or college choices while they're still young, naturally we'll have to wait for the answers.

Let's begin praying future prayers now.

Catherine, a young praying mother, wrote her "waiting prayers" on egg-shaped pieces of paper, slipped them into her Bible and prayed, "Lord, You hatch these prayers in Your perfect timing." Some fifteen years later when she acquired a beautiful Christian daughter-in-law, she rejoiced over the wonderful fruit of her "waiting prayers."

We who sow "waiting prayers" should consider the wise gardener who plants tiny seeds and has the good sense not to dig them up every few days to see if a crop is on the way. Instead, let's wait for God to bring the answers in His own good time.

In addition to these suggestions, I've stumbled over other exciting, profitable ways to pray. They haven't always come easily. Some have come by trial and error, others by weeping and travailing. Occasionally verses from the Bible seem to leap off

15

the page at me to become my own personal prayers. Bargaining prayers, I've learned, are not acceptable.

"Mothers are the best intercessors because they love more and hurt more," a wise man once wrote.

Mothers like the Virgin Mary are "God-bearers." From us, children first hear about God and learn their first prayers. May we grasp what a special privilege, yes, a peculiar advantage we have to pray for our children, grandchildren, nieces, nephews, and for the neighborhood children. It doesn't matter how old these children are; God loves them and wants none of them to perish.

My own son's affirmation of my prayers the summer he was a lifeguard taught me what a privilege it is to pray for our youngsters.

TWO

Praying for Our Households

"Believe in the Lord Jesus, and you will be saved—you and your household" (Acts 16:31).

How many of us have read that scripture, sighed, and said, "Oh, if only that were true in my life. If only my belief in the Lord could assure that my entire household would be saved!"

"What must I do to be saved?" the Philippian jailer asked Paul and Silas after the Lord had supernaturally freed them from their prison stocks. *"Believe in the Lord Jesus, and you will be saved—you and your household,"* they replied (Acts 16:31). That very night the jailer and all his household believed.

Paul gave further hope to Christians when he wrote that an unbelieving husband or wife is sanctified by a believing partner. *"Otherwise your children would be unclean [unblessed heathen, outside the Christian covenant], but as it is they are prepared for God—pure and clean" (1 Cor. 7:14 TAB).*

A parent can speak for the household as illustrated by Joshua's

17

statement: *"But as for me and my household, we will serve the Lord" (Josh. 24:15).*

Salvation for a whole household had its beginnings in the Old Testament. In Exodus chapter 12, God gave Passover-night instructions when He told the Israelites He was going to bring them out of Egypt, *"Each man is to take a lamb for his family, one for each household" (v. 3).* The lamb's blood on the doorposts prevented the destroyer from coming into the houses of His chosen people. Today we know that the Lamb of the Passover is Jesus Christ and that we are the spiritual Israelites. When we are in right relationship with Him, our household is included in His promises.

Even as the early Jews, we must keep His words before our families, *"Teach and impress them diligently upon the [minds and] hearts of your children" (Deut. 6:7 TAB).* When we do this, we can expect God to do His part and draw our children to Himself.

Another Old Testament scripture offers assurance for our families: *"I will pour out my Spirit on all people."* When Joel speaks of sons and daughters, young and old men, and servants, he is talking about whole households (Joel 2:28,29).

When we read, *"The promise is for you and your children" (Acts 2:39),* we need to keep in mind that this refers to both our present households and to future generations.

When parents brought their little children to Jesus to have Him lay hands on them, the disciples rebuked them. Jesus was indignant. *"Let the little children come to me, and do not hinder them, for the kingdom of God belongs to such as these,"* He said. *"I tell you the truth, anyone who will not receive the kingdom of God like a little child will never enter it" (Mark 10:14,15).*

Jesus took the children in His arms, put His hands on them, and blessed them.

I understand this "blessing" was a Jewish custom on the Day

of Atonement. Babies and children were brought by their parents to the elders and scribes for prayer and blessing.

Perhaps the disciples thought that Jesus didn't want to continue that custom. But He said, "Let them come and don't keep them away." Jesus accepted and blessed the children. In a sense, He was reaffirming the spiritual covenant God had made with their parents, recognizing children as a part of the covenant household.

And so it is with us when we obey God's Word.

The following verses have encouraged a number of praying parents. Ask God to make them real to you:

1. *"The promise is for you and your children and for all who are far off—for all whom the Lord our God will call" (Acts 2:39).*

2. *"All your sons will be taught by the Lord, and great will be your children's peace" (Isa. 54:13).*

3. *"I will pour out My Spirit on your offspring, and my blessing on your descendants" (Isa. 44:3).*

4. *"The seed of the righteous shall be delivered" (Prov. 11:21 KJV).*

5. *"He will deliver even one who is not innocent, who will be delivered through the cleanness of your hands" (Job. 22:30).*

6. *"'As for me, this is my covenant with them,' says the Lord. 'My Spirit, who is on you, and my words that I have put in your mouth will not depart from your mouth, or from the mouths of your children, or from the mouths of their descendants from this time on and forever,' says the Lord" (Isa. 59:21).*

7. *"But from everlasting to everlasting the Lord's love is with those who fear him, and his righteousness with their children's children" (Ps. 103:17).*

19

Three

Surrendering Our Children

"Sons are a heritage from the Lord, children a reward from him" (Ps. 127:3).

A pastor paused midway in the wedding ceremony he was conducting for his son, looked out across the sanctuary, cleared his throat and said, "My friends, I have something I want to share with you. This afternoon my wife and I brought all our children down to the church altar. As they knelt here, we literally gave all five back to God. Since our first child is now leaving home, we told the Lord, 'We realize we are only caretakers of these children. We dedicate them once and for all to You.'"

I squirmed in my seat. I'd never heard anything like this before, certainly not at a wedding.

"God says in His Word," the pastor continued, "that children are a heritage from Him. I look on ours as gifts entrusted to us for awhile."

For several days I couldn't shake what he's said about dedicating his children to God. I remembered clearly the occasions when my husband and I presented our three babies for christening. But had we dedicated them to God?

Some weeks after that wedding while I was reading the Old Testament, a passage seemed to leap from the page into my heart. It was Hannah's "surrender prayer" to God for her little boy Samuel. *"Now I give him to the Lord. For his whole life he will be given over to the Lord" (I Sam. 1:28)*.

Touched by this, I stopped my reading and repeated the prayer as my own, inserting the names of our three children. There, I thought, I've given them back to God.

Little did I know what a test I'd go through some nine years later when Keith, our college-age son, was missing at sea. As we gazed across the black white-capped waves late that summer evening, my husband grabbed my arm and prayed, "God, You know we've dedicated Keith to You. He was baptized in this very gulf at his own request two years ago. We commit him totally to You—dead or alive."

My heart pled, "Oh, Jesus don't let him be dead. Find him for us."

As I walked the beach and prayed, I finally came to a point where I could surrender him unconditionally to his Creator. How thankful I was when he was found safe before daybreak.

Vicky, a South Dakota mother of seven, wrote to me about her "surrender" experience. "A little more than a year after I had been born again," she said, "my husband and I faced a crucial problem with the increasing misbehavior and disobedience of our fourteen-year-old son. We talked to him, reasoned with him, and punished him with little visible effect. His mind was like solid concrete. One evening as I was preparing for bed, I sat down on the edge of the bathtub and said, 'God, there is nothing more my husband and I know to do for this child. I give him over to You—completely."

Vicky calls it "total release." Within three weeks, the impossible situation her son had gotten himself into was resolved. "Undoubtedly, God moved on our behalf," she said. "This child was one of the first to ask Jesus to be his Savior. In fact, within six months my entire family, including my husband, seven children, two of their spouses, and one fiancee were all saved and filled with the Holy Spirit. It was not my elaborate prayers. But it was God's Word fulfilled in the life of a believer. *'The prayer of a righteous man (or woman) is powerful and effective,'* we read in James 5:16," she concluded.

Dedicating our children to God carries great responsibilities. It means we'll not only depend on the Lord to help us raise them, but also we will accept those children just as God made them.

I have met some mothers—even Christians—who have deep resentments toward their children. One baby disrupted his mother's promising professional career; another child brought his mother such heartache that she inwardly hated him. "I wish I'd never had him," she cried.

Jesus tells us that if we want our prayers answered, we must forgive.

"When you stand praying, if you hold anything against anyone, forgive him, so that your Father in heaven may forgive you your sins" (Mark 11:25).

It's never too late to honestly ask God to forgive our resentment, lack of acceptance, or failure to love a child. He never asks us to do something without giving us the power to do it. So we also can ask Him to give us His love for those children.

Christ commanded: *"Love each other as I have loved you....Then the Father will give you whatever you ask in my name" (John 15:12,16).*

We learn to pray for our children by (1) giving them back to God, (2) forgiving them, and (3) loving them.

You might want to use a simple thought-exercise to let your

child go. Picture Jesus in your mind. See your child—small or grownup—with Him. They may walk down a dusty road together, Jesus with His arm around your child. Picture them sitting under a tree talking or walking toward the lake to fish. Set your own scene. But see Jesus caring for that child's every need and a warm, personal relationship flowing between the two. You back away. Leave your child there.

A Christian therapist, whose home fellowship members use this dedication prayer for their children, sent it to me to share.

Dedication

Father God, united with You by the birth, death, and resurrection of Your Son Jesus and united as one in our marriage:

1. We thank You for our children _____

_____ .

2. We ask for forgiveness for all sins of omission and com-

mission against _____.

3. We receive this forgiveness and reject any accusation, condemnation, or guilt from Satan.

4. We now break any satanic curse or accusation that has caused bondage to our children. We do this in the authority and by the power of Jesus Christ.

5. In faith, we release them to Your watchcare. Amen.

Note: If you are the only believing parent in your household, you too have the authority to pray this for your children.

Four

Praying Effectively

"When you pray, go into your room, close the door and pray to your Father, who is unseen. Then your Father, who sees what is done in secret, will reward you" (Matt. 6:6).

Do you have a secret place where you go to be alone with God—a special chair, a garden spot, a private nook, a corner desk?

The Gospels frequently tell us of Christ's going into solitude for prayer. *"He went up on a mountainside by himself to pray" (Matt. 14:23).* Luke mentions Jesus' praying eleven times.

We, too, must sit alone in the Father's presence before we can be open channels of intercession for our children. Solitude and quiet help us pray more effectively.

In the Bible we find several other keys to effective prayer:

Know God's Will
"This is the confidence we have in approaching God: that if

24

we ask anything according to his will, he hears us. And if we know that he hears us—whatever we ask—we know that we have what we asked of him" (1 John 5:14,15).

How do we know God's will? By reading and meditating on His Word. In it the Lord says, for example, that it is not the Father's will *"that any...should be lost" (see Matthew 18:14).* So we pray in faith for our children to become believers, knowing this is in line with God's perfect will.

Believe He Hears and Answers Our Prayers

Jesus tells us: *"Whatever you ask for in prayer, believe that you have received it, and it will be yours" (Mark 11:24).*

Pray in Jesus' Name

Jesus assures us, *"I tell you the truth, my Father will give you whatever you ask in my name" (John 16:23).*

Now we can enter triumphantly into our prayer time with Him. I am more convinced than ever of the need to set aside a specific time each day to be with the Lord. I started with just fifteen minutes, expanded it to thirty, and before long I was wanting to lengthen it even further.

As active wives, mothers, and grandmothers, we sometimes complain we don't have time to pray. We send up "minute prayers" like spiritual arrows while we sit at our office desks, iron clothes, drive carpools, or sit in waiting rooms. These prayers are commendable, but God wants some quality time with us each day, too.

Whatever time we set aside for Him—morning, noon, or evening, it helps to have a few tools on hand such as paper, pen, and a Bible. We'll then be able to record our prayers and God's answers. No "quiet time" is complete until we've not only talked but listened to hear our Father's voice. Since we are all different, no two of us will use the same techniques in our personal devo-

25

tional times.

Prayer has no set formulas, but I have found some practical helps that have enriched my private prayer times with God. Perhaps they will help you, too:

Practical Helps

I keep a personal "prayer book," a seven-by-nine-inch loose-leaf notebook, which I fill with prayer requests, words of praise, reports of answered prayers, and specific points I'm learning through prayer or Bible reading. I'm continually removing and replacing these pages.

On the first page I've attached a picture of our family—one taken after an Easter Sunday service when we all were dressed in our best and wore radiant smiles. This is a positive image I want to keep always before me and the Lord. Underneath our picture, I've written a paraphrase of a scripture I pray daily for our family:

"That the God of our Lord Jesus Christ, the glorious Father, may give [us] the Spirit of wisdom and revelation, so that [we] may know Him better" (Eph. 1:17).

Next is an individual page for each family member. At the top I write Scripture prayers as well as practical prayers I'm praying for that child daily. I often record the date beside the request. Later I add the day and the way God answered. This has taught me much about God's perfect timing.

If I'm praying for a daughter away from home who needs a new apartment with lots of storage space, I bring that before the Lord and daily thank Him that He will provide her need. When He does, I write, "Thank You, Lord," and scratch that petition. This exercise boosts my faith.

My notebook is divided into different days of the week so I can pray for friends, government officials, missionaries, relatives, and unsaved friends. Because I'm a visual person, I've pasted photos or pictures from magazines of many I pray for during the week, such as the president, supreme court justices, and foreign leaders. I am not a slave to this notebook or method. It's just a helpful vehicle I keep beside my Bible for my daily appointment with the Lord.

During this private time, God sometimes speaks to me through my Bible reading. Once during a personal trial with one of our youngsters, I read about the disciples' calling out for Jesus' help as their boat was lashed by a raging storm.

"Where is your faith?" He asked them.

Yes, I thought, where was their faith? Jesus had told them to get into the boat, and they'd go over to the other side of the lake. His word was trustworthy, wasn't it? Wasn't He along with them? Why were they worried?

Then the Lord spoke to my spirit: "Where is your faith? Haven't I promised you that all your children will be taught of the Lord? Haven't I said I'd bring them back from the land of the enemy? Don't you trust Me with the plans I have for them? I will give them a future and not calamity."

How my heart was pierced!

Actually, those were verses that had lain dormant in my heart for a long time, and I needed them brought back to my memory. Of course, the Lord had promised. And in a sense He's always "in my boat" despite my turbulent storms.

One reason I like to quote Scripture verses aloud as prayers is because God has promised that His Word will not return empty or void. It will accomplish what He intends (see Isaiah 55:11). Speaking His Word aloud builds my faith in the One who works all things to my good and the good of my children, too.

You may want to get a notebook and write down any impressions the Lord gives you during your time with Him. If you've never done it before, you'll find it exciting.

A pastor's wife I know tried this idea with her prayers for

her rebellious teenage daughter Susan. She asked God to show her how to love Susan and to teach the girl how to respond to that love.

Whenever little thoughts came to her that were related to Susan, she wrote them down in a spiral notebook, such as, "Don't go grocery shopping until Susan can go with you. Don't buy Susan's clothes until she can help you select them. Let Susan help you cook supper. Choose some of her favorite dishes."

These may sound insignificant, but as this mother began to do them, she saw a softening in Susan. Gradually, Susan's attitude changed and so did her appearance. Her body slimmed down and her personality blossomed. It was not an overnight miracle by any means but a slow metamorphosis.

The mother had learned a significant lesson: "God didn't take away Susan's self-will; He just converted it into what He put it there for in the first place," she says. "She turned her life over to the Lord completely and became strong in her convictions. In fact, she is no longer rebellious or easily led astray by her peers but instead is counseling many of her troubled friends."

Today Susan is happily married to a fine Christian and can hardly remember that troubled period in her life.

Oh, what special moments await us in our secret times of prayer. How our Father longs to hear our prayers for our children.

Let me share two prayers of Mrs. Johnnie Lord, a pastor's wife.

"Lord, I want Your love to be free today to flow through me, so fill my mind with ways to reach out in love to my family members, _____."

* * * * *

"God, what do You want me to trust You for today in the lives of my children?" (Write ideas down as they come.)

* * * * *

28

Below are some Scripture intercessions that I pray for my children:

Dedication
Lord, as You did for Hannah, take this child of mine,

_____. I give him/her to You. For his/her whole life, he/she will be given over to You (1 Sam. 1:28).

Salvation
Father, You are not willing that _____

should be lost, but that this child come to repentance. Lord Jesus, I thank You that You came to save the lost, including

_____and me. I thank You in advance that

_____will become a believer in You (Matt. 18:14; 2 Pet. 3:9).

Deliverance
Father, I thank You that You will deliver _____

from the evil one and guide him in paths of righteousness for Your name's sake (Matt. 6:13; Ps. 23:3).

Forgiveness
Thank You, Father, that the blood of Jesus purifies us from

all sin. Thank You that _____has asked for your

forgiveness and cleansing. Now help _____

forget what is behind and strain toward what is ahead, pressing on toward the goal to win the prize for which God has called him/her heavenward in Christ Jesus (1 John 1:7,9; Phil. 3:13,14).

Future

I thank You, Lord, that You know the plans You have for

_____, to prosper and not to harm him/her, to

give _____ hope and a future. I pray

that _____ will not walk in the counsel of the

wicked, or stand in the way of sinners, or sit in the seat of

mockers. But I pray that _____ 's delight

will be in the law of the Lord and that he/she will meditate on it day and night (Jer. 29:11; Ps. 1).

Health

Father, I thank You that Jesus took our infirmities and carried our sorrows. And thank You by His wounds, we are healed.

I pray that in all respects _____ may enjoy

good health and that all may go well with him/her, even as his/her soul is getting along well. I thank You for Your prom-

ise to sustain _____ on his/her sickbed and restore

_____ from his/her bed of illness

(Isa. 53:4,5; 3 John 2; Ps. 41:3).

Life's Work

Lord, fill _____ with the knowledge

of Your will through all spiritual wisdom and understanding, so that he/she lives a life worthy of You, to please You in every way (Col. 1:9,10).

Maturity

Dear Father, may _____, like Your

Son Jesus, grow in wisdom and stature, and in favor with You

and with the people his/her life touches. Give_____

a listening ear to parental instructions. Help him/her to pay attention that he/she may gain understanding (Luke 2:52; Prov. 4:1).

Needs

Thank You, dear Father, that You will supply all of

_____'s needs according to Your glorious riches

in Christ Jesus (Phil. 4:19).

Protection

Thank You, dear God, that You will command Your angels

concerning _____ to guard him/her in

all his/her ways (Ps. 91:11).

Spiritual Growth

Father, give _____the Spirit of wisdom and reve-

lation, so that he/she may know You better. I pray that the eyes of his/her heart may be enlightened in order that he/she may know the hope to which You have called him/her, the riches of Your glorious inheritance in the saints, and Your incomparably great power for us who believe. I pray that Christ may dwell in his/her heart through faith and that he/she may be rooted and established in love (Eph. 1:17-19; 3:17).

Temptation

Thank You, dear Father, that You know how to rescue

_____from temptation and trials. I pray that

_____will flee the evil desires of youth, and pursue

righteousness, faith, love, and peace, along with those who call on You out of a pure heart. I pray that he/she will not have anything to do with stupid arguments, because we know they

produce quarrels. I ask that _____

will keep his way pure by living according to Your Word, hiding it in his/her heart (2 Pet. 2:9; 2 Tim. 2:22,23; Ps. 119:9-11).

General

Lord, with thanksgiving I present my requests to You today

on behalf of my children, _____

_____ .

(Name the requests). I speak them with my mouth, believe them with my heart, and thank You in advance for hearing me. I pray in Jesus' name (Phil. 4:6; Mark 11:23).

Prayer for My Daughter's Future Partner

Lord, may he love the Lord with all his heart, soul, mind, and strength, and Jesus as his personal Lord and Savior (Mark 12:29,30; Rom. 10:9).

May he love his wife with a faithful, undying love for as long as they both shall live (Matt. 19:5,6).

May he recognize his body as the temple of the Holy Spirit and treat it wisely (1 Cor. 16:19,20). May he be healthy, able to work and support a family (1 Tim. 6:8).

May he have an admirable goal in life (Matt. 6:33).

May he use his talents wisely and release his wife to use her God-given talents, also. May their talents complement one another. May they enjoy doing things together (Matt. 25:1,14-30).

May he establish their home in accordance with God's prescribed order as outlined in Ephesians 5:20-28.

May he be strong in mind. May the two of them be compatible intellectually (2 Cor. 13:11; 1 Tim. 1:7).

May he be a good money manager (1 Tim. 5:8; 6:10).

Lord, bring this partner into my daughter's life in Your perfect timing. May she be so in love with him and he with her and both of them in love with You, O God, that there will be no doubt that You created them for each other as long as they both shall live.

In Jesus' name, amen.

Prayer for My Son's Partner

Lord, may they be equally yoked (2 Cor. 6:14).

May she love the Lord God with all her heart, soul, mind, and strength. May she embrace Jesus as her personal Savior and Lord (Mark 12:29,30; Rom. 10:9).

May she love my son with an undying love as long as they both shall live and be a helper suitable for him (Gen. 2:18).

May she be rich in good deeds, generous, and hospitable (1 Tim. 6:18; Heb. 13:2).

May she encourage my son daily (Heb. 3:13).

May she use her God-given talents at home and in Your kingdom's work (Matt. 25:14-30).

If housework ever seems to be a monotonous chore to her, help her realize that whatever she does in word or deed, she should do it with all her heart as working for You (Col. 3:17,23).

When they have a family, help her be a good mother. May her children arise and call her blessed (Tit. 2:4,5; Prov. 31:28).

Show her how to prepare nutritious meals for her family. If she needs to learn something about homemaking, don't let her be shy about asking more mature Christian women to help her (Tit. 2:3-5).

(P.S. Help me be a good mother-in-law to this precious one.)
In Jesus' name, amen.

My Prayer Journal

Here are some entries from my prayer journal over the years.

Heal her broken heart

Lord, our daughter's heart is broken. Comfort her. It was her first touch of love, and now he's dumped her for another girl. Her pride is wounded. She feels rejected, worth nothing. Oh, Lord, may she realize You love her and we love her. Heal her hurts. Bring other Christian friends into her life who can help fill the void left after losing her special friend. Help her get her priorities in order and realize her real purpose in life should be to love and please You. Thank You for Your everlasting arms around our daughter—Your daughter.

Help with exam

Lord, he has an important exam today. He's studied long and hard. Yet, he's anxious, with butterflies inside. Quiet his spirit. Bring to his mind all the things he's studied and stored away for this moment. Help him to do his best. Thank You, Lord.

Help her accept herself

Lord, our daughter is almost two heads taller than the other girls in her class. She feels like a giant. Show her You made her just like she is for a purpose. You know what You have in store for her not only in her physical makeup but with the abilities You have given her. She's struggling hard right now to find her true identity. Please help her see she is special and unique, just as each of Your children is.

Help me be an encourager

Lord, he's not doing well in school as I'd like. Help me accept his pace. Though I'd like better grades, keep me from pushing him beyond his capacity. Show me how to encourage him, right where he is.

Let him forgive me

Today I lost my cool and said some cutting things I wish I could take back. I hurt my son with words. As I ask him to forgive me, restore our relationship, Lord. Help me know when to correct and when to keep silent. Lord, I want to manifest the fruits of Your Spirit in my life—love, joy, peace, patience, kindness, goodness, faithfulness, gentleness, and self-control.

Draw her back

God, I watch so helplessly as our teenager drifts away from You. You know we gave this child to You at birth. I remember when I was a teen. I, too, questioned and rebelled. But in Your loving time, You drew me back to You, stronger, firmer, more sure than ever of the reality of the risen Lord, my Savior. Do so with our child. O God, do so again. Thank You that You do answer mothers' prayers.

Marriage partner

Lord, make it clear to him if she's the one to be his helpmate. Help them both grow up in You, Lord. Cut off their rough edges so they'll be ready for marriage. If they are to be life partners, thank You. If not, take her away from him without rejection or wounding.

Demonstrate your greatness

Today is a big day on the job for her—a day to make a presentation before the bosses. Move in a mighty way on her behalf, Lord God of hosts. Demonstrate Your greatness in her life that others may see You, Lord. Protect her body, mind, and spirit.

Moving prayers

She's anticipating a job change in a couple of months. O, Lord, lead her to the job of Your choice in the town of Your choice where she can use her education, skills, and ability to the best capacity. Continue to release Your flow of creativity in her. Guide her, too, to the right church, right roommates, and right apartment complex. I give You thanks in advance, for You are a faithful, loving Father. Thank You that this adult child of mine continues to love and serve You with her gifts.

Accomplish your will

Today accomplish Your will in my children's lives, Father. Have mercy on them according to Your loving-kindness.

Two job offers

Lord, it hardly seems possible. When we prayed for a new job for him, he got two good offers. Give him wisdom and discernment to make the right choice. Thank You, Lord.

Praise for answered prayer

Last September while I was in church You showed me in my mind's eye all three of our children with arms uplifted praising

You, Lord. I wrote in my prayer journal that I accepted that picture and would stand in faith until it was fulfilled. Today in looking back over my prayer journal, I was reminded again how faithful You are. After only eight months, You've brought all three into a deeper commitment, a closer walk. Indeed, they are singing Your praises with uplifted arms. Oh, thank You, Lord. Thank You, Lord.

Five

Two in Agreement

"Again, I tell you that if two of you on earth agree about anything you ask for, it will be done for you by my Father in heaven. For where two or three come together in my name, there am I with them" (Matt. 18:19,20).

When we are serious about praying for our children, we soon realize what sources of strength and encouragement prayer partners can be. Not only do we help carry each other's burdens, but we rejoice together over answered prayers. Every Christian needs a special friend who will share her secret problems, needs, and concerns and never divulge them to anyone but the Lord.

The word *agree* in Greek is *sumphoneo,* which gives us in English the word *symphony*—musical harmony. Loosely translated it means: "If two of you can harmonize (have harmony in the Spirit) concerning anything that you ask, it will be done."

Harvey and Yvonne Hester pray daily for their two teenage

38

daughters. In the morning before the girls leave for school, they ask God's blessing, direction, and protection for them. Sometimes at night while the girls sleep, their parents stand over their beds and pray for them again.

"If one is having a battle with fear, we'll pray a scripture like, *"God did not give us a spirit of fear"* (2 Tim. 1:7 KJV), explained Harvey, a clinical member of the American Association for Marriage and Family Therapy. This Florida couple say they've prayed for their children since before conception.

Our Christian husbands are ideal prayer partners if they're willing and available. Single mothers or wives with unbelieving husbands obviously lack this needed "support system." That's why trusted women prayer partners are gifts indeed.

For a period of years I had two prized, dependable prayer partners. Since Lib was my age, we both had children of similar ages. While they were going through the "terrible teens," we supported each other in prayer over the phone almost every weekday. Believe me, we learned new depths of prayer as we went through several crises with our youngsters—car wrecks, illnesses, hospital emergency-room trips, small brushes with the law, even runaways.

Laura, at the other end of the scale, was five years ahead of me physically and spiritually. Though we lived forty miles apart, we met twice a month to pray either at her home or mine. She was my encourager, my affirmer. "Hey, you're going to make it," she'd often say, laughing about a situation that looked hopeless to me. "Listen, one of my kids went through that kind of agony. I'll pray you through this. Believe me, it's not as gloomy as you think."

When one of my children was falsely accused, Laura brought me back on course, "That's simply out of character for your child. Don't you believe a lie from the devil. We'll pray and ask God to reveal the truth." She stood in the gap for me for two years until the Lord proved the accuser was wrong.

Since two of her children were married, I had the privilege of praying for her sons-in-law and grandchildren.

I've since moved far from Lib and Laura, but we still exchange prayer requests by phone or letter. After all, we have too many hours invested in our prayer lives together to let distance keep us apart spiritually.

After we moved, it was some time before I found two new prayer partners. Again, I have a mature friend Fran who brings balance and wisdom to my prayer life. Then there's Carol who prays with me with keen identity since her children are in college or about to launch into their own careers. With these two women I am specific about my prayer concerns, telling them anything that's on my heart, confident they'll share only with the Lord. In turn, I pray for them through good and trying times.

We've already been through a couple of traumas. Three years ago, for instance, Fran's son almost died of cancer. Then last year Carol, who had already lost one child in a car wreck, spent several months on a hospital cot beside her sixteen-year-old daughter who had broken her neck in a smashup. How we praised God for their recoveries.

Other friends are available when I need to call and say, "We'd like you to pray with us that God will bring victory into our child's life." Sometimes I don't even mention the specific problem or situation.

By far, my best prayer colleague is my husband. Every day we pray aloud for our children, calling each by name.

"How can you get your husband to pray with you?" women often ask. I usually suggest what other wives have told me worked for them when their husbands were reluctant.

A woman might say to her husband, "Honey, do you mind if I pray aloud for the children while you say 'amen' in agreement with me?" Eventually he'll get the idea that prayer is just conversation with the Father.

Or if our husbands are not sure how to pray aloud, we can give them some Scripture prayers that they can read aloud while we agree.

"Pray aloud?" one mother questioned me, wrinkling her brow in a look of total bewilderment.

I knew where she was coming from, because I'd been there myself. I had to learn to pray aloud. My friend Laura encouraged me to get used to hearing my own voice speaking aloud in prayer.

I have become even freer in prayer since I've joined an early-morning group of six women to intercede for our families once a week. By listening to them pray and praise, I now understand prayer much better.

Our group meets on Monday mornings from 5:30-6:30. When the others return to their homes to get husbands and children off to work and school, Fran and I stay to pray over our concerns. Right now this schedule works for us, because my husband leaves for work at 5:30 and hers is retired and still asleep.

If we don't have prayer partners, we can ask God for them. Even Jesus had an inner circle of praying friends—Peter, James, and John—who went apart with Him on occasion.

Six

Praying for Our Children's Friends

"And the Lord turned the captivity of Job when he prayed for his friends" (Job 42:10 KJV).

Another priceless privilege that comes with praying for our children is praying for their friends, too.

Psychologists agree that nobody influences a teenager—negatively or positively—like his peers. Usually a young person is introduced to his first drug experience by his or her "best" friend. However, a caring friend may also save his life. We need to pray for the right friends to come into our children's lives.

One mother learned a new way to pray after she'd almost lost hope for her high-school son Kurt who was being led down a path of destruction by his friend Teddy.

"It was Teddy who was in favor of skipping Sunday school class and slipping out of church," she said. "He even bought the bottle of wine they guzzled down the night we found Kurt passed out on his bed." Large for his age, Teddy had no trouble buying wine from a convenience store.

"The alcohol made them both as sick as overstuffed pups. We hoped and prayed the hangover and lecture my husband gave them would have an effect. But they kept on with their pranks. I had to face the fact that our son had a will of his own and that he chose to do whatever Teddy suggested. They fed each other's bad points when they were together. I was concerned, too, because Kurt had dropped his other close friends just to be at Teddy's beck and call," the mother continued.

Then one night when Kurt was supposed to be studying, he took the family car and picked Teddy up for a ride in the country. They'd barely gotten out of the city limits when another car collided with Kurt's sending him to the hospital with multiple cuts and bruises.

Kurt's parents punished, lectured, pleaded, cried, prayed. And prayed some more. They tried to reason with Kurt and Teddy together, then separately. They even tried to enlist the help of Teddy's mom. Nothing worked, not even forbidding the boys to see each other. They just arranged to meet secretly.

Teddy graduated from high school but enrolled at a nearby community college, making it easy for the two boys to continue seeing one another.

When Kurt's mom had prayed every prayer she knew, she finally asked God to show her how to pray. Lying across her bed one evening reading the Bible, she came to a verse in the last chapter of Job. *"The Lord turned (broke) the captivity of Job when he prayed for his friends,"* she read aloud to her husband lying beside her. "That's what's been missing in our prayers," she exclaimed. "I think God wants us to pray for Teddy as much as for Kurt!"

"Fine. You pray and I'll agree," he told her.

They asked God to bless, prosper, and direct Teddy. No longer did they ask Him to remove this boy from their son's life. They prayed a "blessing" prayer for Teddy every day.

Two weeks later Kurt came bounding into the kitchen where his mom was peeling vegetables for supper. "Guess what?" he asked, swiping a carrot off the countertop. "Teddy's got a baseball scholarship and is going to college up north."

"But this is late January," she said, laying down her knife. "I didn't know they passed out scholarships in midterm."

"All I know is he got a phone call telling him he's got one, and he's leaving right away. The college is about a thousand miles from here."

God had broken the captivity.

Kurt's parents could hardly believe how quickly God had answered their prayers for Teddy's best. Not only was he blessed with college tuition, but he was being temporarily removed from their son's life.

Today both young men love the Lord Jesus—both met Him later in college.

"I learned a great lesson from that: I pray for all the close friends of my children. I also learned to ask God *how* to pray for those friends," the mother said.

Another mother, whose son smoked pot whenever he got around a certain group of boys, always prayed the same verse whenever she came to our church's prayer group: "Lord, keep my son from the traps set for him by evildoers. Let the wicked fall into their own nets, while he passes by in safety," which is a paraphrase of Psalm 141:9,10. When she stopped praying it, I asked her about it.

"It was just a scripture I was led to pray. Those boys leave him alone now, so I don't pray it anymore."

Christ told us to bless those who curse us and to pray for those who mistreat us. Admittedly, it is difficult to know when to pray for God to remove a person who has a bad influence on your child and when to pray for his best. That's why it is important to ask God how to pray.

Remember we said a good friend can have a positive influence on our children, too? In *Changepoints,* author Joyce Landorf tells about the blind trust she had to maintain during several years of a deteriorating relationship with her daughter Laurie.

One day when Laurie had made up her mind to elope with a young man her parents knew was not a suitable mate for her, she dropped by her friend Gayle's house to let her in on the news. Gayle reminded her that she'd always talked about a big wedding with her mother singing "Sunrise, Sunset." That convinced Laurie and she didn't elope.

"Mr. Right," who had been waiting in the wings for three years, finally got Laurie's attention. When the couple was married nine months later, Joyce Landorf sang "Sunrise, Sunset" as Laurie came down the aisle.

Joyce was glad that for years she'd prayed for one Christian peer person who would hold her child's head above water. Gayle turned out to be that one.

No matter how old our children are, they are influenced by peer pressure. Yes, it is important for us to pray for their friends.

Here are two prayers we can pray:

Lord, we bless and thank You for our children's friends. May they be good influences upon each other. We know Your Word says bad company corrupts morals. Guard our children from wrong friends, wrong influences, and wrong environments. In Jesus' name we ask this, amen.

* * * * *

Lord, counteract the influence of the world on my children. Keep them from being misled by wrong peer groups. Plant Your Word in their hearts. Keep me from bitterness when I see them rebel. Give me patience to wait upon Your timing. Show me how to be merciful and gracious even as Jesus was, amen.

Seven

Praying for Those in Authority over Our Children

"I urge, then, first of all, that requests, prayers, intercession and thanksgiving be made for everyone—for kings and all those in authority, that we may live peaceful and quiet lives in all godliness and holiness" (1 Tim. 2:1,2).

In praying for our children—whether they live at home or away—do we remember to pray for those in authority over them?

I'd never thought much about praying for my children's teachers until I heard a pastor stress the need to pray for *all* those in authority over us.

My three youngsters were in different schools with six teachers each. I couldn't possibly know them all personally. But I could lift them up to the Lord in a general way.

Not long after I'd added them to my prayer list, our son Keith got a telephone call during our supper hour from one of his teachers.

"What did she want?" I asked when he returned to the table.

"Oh, nothing really. She just called to apologize for yelling at me in class today," he said rather nonchalantly.

Something inside wanted to shout, "Thank You, Lord! Thank You for showing me the need to pray for teachers."

Was it my imagination or was there a softening in my children's attitudes toward their teachers after I started praying for them? I was pondering this when our daughter Quinett, who was away for her first year of college, called home unexpectedly at noon one day.

"Mom, my favorite teacher has cancer and is possibly dying. I'm going to the hospital to see her right now. Will you pray for her?" I did right then as she agreed with me.

Along this line, we need to pray for protection from wrong teaching that comes down to our children from worldly or ungodly teachers. How blessed we are when our children learn scriptural principles from godly teachers who are themselves in submission to the Lord.

Now that my children are out in the work world, I've found it equally necessary to pray daily for their employers. Doesn't the Bible admonish us to pray for all in authority?

I also pray about the right jobs for them, like this:

"Lord, may this child get only the job You want him to have. Close doors where You don't want him to go. I thank You in Jesus' name, amen."

I recall the first time I prayed that for Keith. It was the summer before his senior year of high school, and he'd looked everywhere he knew for a job in our small community. Nothing seemed open. Of course, I was praying God would keep doors closed where He didn't want Keith to be. Finally, our pastor told him of a janitorial job in an industrial park. He accepted it, even though he didn't like the sound of the working hours—from 6 p.m. until 2 a.m.

But it proved to be one of Keith's best summers ever. He was free in the daytime to surf in the Atlantic, his favorite pastime. And late at night, when he was cleaning windows, mopping floors, and vacuuming carpets, Christian men who worked with him talked to him about tithing, giving, praying, and other spiritual topics we'd often discussed at our family devotions. Somehow this talk had a strong impact coming from men in the work world. How I thanked God for that job and for that special employer who hired Christians.

Today Keith has graduated from college, packed his bags, loaded a small trailer of furniture, and moved to a city four hundred miles away where he thinks he wants to live. As he looks for the right job, I'm praying, "Lord, open the right doors. Give him a good boss who will give him godly counsel."

One summer I prayed a "door-opener" prayer for his sister Sherry, only to see unexpected results. The job she landed was as a desk clerk at a beach resort hotel. Soon I sensed something was wrong at work. Six weeks later Sherry came home in the middle of the morning. She'd lost her job. What a blow!

Hadn't we prayed and asked God for just the right job? Yes. Hadn't it been a job that tied in with her planned college major? Yes? What then had gone wrong?

As Sherry fell across her bed crying, I lay beside her, stroking her hair and turning over in my mind some of the negatives of her job. She had had to handle several thousand of dollars in cash each night, then deliver it to the keeper of the safe in the next building. A bit risky for a seventeen-year-old. Down the beach two employees had recently been murdered during a robbery. Then, too, an employee her own age had seemed bent on keeping the office in turmoil. I'd prayed several times with my daughter about this troubled girl.

While I was offering a few words of encouragement, my husband poked his head in the door, took one look at us sprawled across the bed, and asked me, "How have you been praying for Sherry?"

"Well, you know that every day I ask for the Lord to protect her from evil environment, evil influences, and evil people."

"Then why are you surprised she lost her job? Can't you see God's protection over her?"

I got my thinking back in perspective in a hurry!

After the initial humiliation, Sherry forced herself to go job hunting again. Within a week she found one. We had almost forgotten about her first job until the next summer when her former employer asked her to come back to the beach hotel. As she had another job waiting, she declined.

Had God opened the eyes of this former employer to Sherry's true worth? Perhaps we'll never find out, but it was gracious of the Lord to let us know she had been vindicated in the man's eyes.

Painful as it was, we had learned a valuable lesson. Now we can sympathize more readily with those who go through similar disappointments. Surely, our heartaches are a time of learning and training for future usefulness. But in this instance, we believe we also experienced God's divine protection.

As I think about that particular employer, I can praise God because his wife is now active in our church's prayer group, and she shares with him at home about answered prayer.

Yes, we can say with the apostle Paul that requests, prayers, intercession, and thanksgiving be made—especially for all those in authority in our lives and the lives of our youngsters, too.

Eight

Praying in the Spirit

"For if I pray in an [unknown] tongue, my spirit [by the Holy Spirit within me] prays" (1 Cor. 14:14 TAB).

The shrill ring of the phone jarred me awake. I switched on the light and glanced at the clock. It read 2 a.m. Realizing it must be an emergency, I started to pray in tongues as I reached for the telephone.

"Hello."

"This is Betty. I hate to bother you at this hour, but I've got an important prayer request." Though groggy from sleep, I recognized my friend's voice. She was one of the handful of praying women I called when I needed support.

"We just got a phone call about our son John. He got some bad drugs, angel dust or something equally dangerous, at the New Orleans rock festival. We begged him not to go, but a twenty-five-year old living away from home doesn't always listen to his parents. A minister friend just called—John is in the

50

psychiatric ward of a hospital there, completely out of his mind. I need prayer for John and for George and me. We're leaving right away for New Orleans."

I prayed briefly with her, then continued in intercessory prayer after she hung up. Over the next two weeks, Betty frequently called our church office to give an update on John's condition. We, her prayer warriors, in turn called the church for progress reports.

"He's writhing and hissing like a snake, his tongue darting in and out of his mouth at a rapid pace as he spits at his dad and me," Betty told our pastor. "Nothing calms him until I sit by his bed and pray in tongues for hours on end."

On her next call, she reported, "It looks like he opened himself up to demonic influences by taking those drugs. The doctors tell us there is no hope. They think he'll be a vegetable all his life. He doesn't even know us."

After three weeks and little improvement, a deputy sheriff and a hospital attendant brought John in a padded wagon to a psychiatric hospital closer to home. Still he had to be tied to a bed to restrain him from physically harming himself or others. Except for the hospital staff, no one but his parents and their minister were allowed in his room. A group from our church continued to pray in support of Betty and George, believing John's mind would be restored.

"John calms down only when I intercede aloud in my prayer language," Betty told me when she phoned. "Then, and only then, does he stop his hissing and tossing."

We continued to pray for the next two months. By now his mom was reading the Bible aloud to him, and John's new medical report showed that his mind was clearing. How we rejoiced a few weeks later when John came home.

One morning soon afterwards, I saw him in the church office where he'd come for counseling.

"John, you look great," I said, wondering to myself if he'd had an inner change.

"Thank you. I know God saved my life through Mom's prayers," he said. "She told me she prayed in tongues for hours when I wasn't even conscious that she was by my bed. I give Jesus all the glory for setting me free." With that, he gave me a big hug.

Three years later his mind remains free and clear. And his mother? She still prays in her prayer language for her three sons every day.

When I simply don't know how to pray for my children in English, my native tongue, I rely on the special prayer language God gave me when I received the baptism in the Holy Spirit. Since my children are away from home and I'm no longer as knowledgeable about their daily needs, I find myself praying more and more in the Spirit.

When I pray in tongues, I'm trusting in the Scripture that says, *"The Spirit intercedes for the saints in accordance with God's will" (Rom. 8:27).*

The apostle Paul gives us some valuable advice in the sixth chapter of Ephesians: *"And pray in the Spirit on all occasions with all kinds of prayers and requests" (v. 18).* That's a tall order!

Reading Romans 8:26-28 in *The Amplified Bible* helps us to understand further.

"So too the (Holy) Spirit comes to our aid and bears us up in our weakness; for we do not know what prayer to offer nor how to offer it worthily as we ought, but the Spirit Himself goes to meet our supplication and pleads in our behalf with unspeakable yearnings and groanings too deep for utterance. And He who searches the hearts of men knows what is in the mind of the (Holy) Spirit—what His intent is—because the Spirit intercedes and pleads [before God] in behalf of the saints according to and in harmony with God's will."

Praying mothers who use their prayer languages on behalf of their children have experienced firsthand God's intervention in those lives. They know, too, that every prayer prayed in the Spirit is a prayer breathed in the will of God.

Nine

Praying during Battle

"For though we live in the world, we do not wage war as the world does. The weapons we fight with are not the weapons of the world. On the contrary, they have divine power to demolish strongholds" (2 Cor. 10:3).

An intercessor sometimes stands between God and a person pleading; at other times, he stands between Satan and a person battling. Someone once said, "Prayer is toward God and warfare toward the enemy."

In Proverbs 31, we read about the virtuous woman who works willingly with her hands. Two kinds of hands mentioned in that often-quoted chapter are *yad* and *kaph* in the Hebrew language.

Kaph hands refer to hands extended to God, beseeching Him on behalf of her loved ones.

Yad hands are warring hands, battling hands. The virtuous, godly woman does warfare with her hands. I picture her balling up her fist and saying, "Satan, you will not have my family.

54

I forbid it by the authority given me by the Lord."

I believe God is calling women to warfare praying. Although we have not fully understood, we are in an army to do battle spiritually. But since Jesus is our commander, we will win! Corrie ten Boom used to say, "It's a poor soldier indeed who does not recognize the enemy."

In this day, when we see a frightening number of our young people who open themselves up to demonic influences through drugs and occult practices, we are more aware than ever that *"we are not fighting against people made of flesh and blood, but against persons without bodies—the evil rulers of the unseen world, those mighty satanic beings and great evil princes of darkness who rule this world; and against huge numbers of wicked spirits in the spirit world" (Eph. 6:12 TLB).*

Paul also reminds us that *"the weapons we fight with are not the weapons of the world. On the contrary, they have divine power to demolish strongholds" (2 Cor. 10:4).*

As Christian mothers, we can battle to demolish strongholds that bind our children by using the powerful weapons found in Revelation 12:11: *"They overcame him by the blood of the Lamb and by the word of their testimony."*

Our authority arises from our right relationship with Jesus—the Lamb who was slain. He in turn gives us the authority in His name to demand that the Evil One turn our children loose.

In warring against Satan and his demonic forces, we can use God's Word as our weapon just as Jesus did when the devil came to tempt Him. Our Lord simply said in effect, "Be gone, Satan, for it is written..." and He went on to quote God's Word.

A mother might battle by saying something comparable to this aloud:

"Be gone, Satan, from my child _____'s

life. You have no authority, because I am a child of God, and

His Word says that the seed of the righteous will be delivered. I'm in covenant relationship with God Almighty through Jesus who died for me. You must release my child."

Scripture tells us, *"Whatever you bind on earth will be bound in heaven, and whatever you loose on earth will be loosed in heaven" (Matt. 16:19).*

What is the meaning of the phrases, "will be bound in heaven...will be loosed in heaven"? Bible translator Williams points out that the verb form indicates something "in a state of having been already forbidden (or permitted)." Thus, whatever is bound or loosed by a believer in accordance with God's will has already been done in heaven.

Jesus further teaches us, *"How can anyone enter a strong man's house and carry off his possessions unless he first ties up the strong man? Then he can rob his house" (Matt. 12:29).*

The context of this passage finds Jesus casting out demons. The Greek word for *bind* in this verse is *deo,* which means "to fasten or tie—as with chains," as an animal is tied to keep it from leaving. We are to bind on earth what has already been bound in heaven.

To what then does the loosing refer? To setting captives free! The Greek word for *loose* is *lud,* defined in the lexicon as "to loose anything tied or fastened; to loose one bound; to set free; to discharge from prison. To free from bondage or disease (one held by Satan) by restoration to health."

Remember the story of Jesus' healing of the woman who'd been crippled by an evil spirit for eighteen years? *"Woman, you are set free from your infirmity,"* the Master told her (Luke 13:12).

Powerful as they are, Satan and demons can be bound; their victims can be set free or loosed by the greater power of God.

Though the devil has an immense kingdom of wicked spirits who carry on his work, the Lord has given us weapons to fight with. It's our responsibility to make war and snatch our children out of the traps Satan has set for them.

Another powerful weapon at our disposal is verbal praise. Satan's fetters are broken when we praise and honor the Most High God (see Ps. 149:6,8).

Reading the Psalms makes us aware that we should praise God whatever our circumstances. No matter what our conditions are, God is worth our praise. Before Jesus left the Passover meal with His disciples to go to Gethsemane and His agony, He sang a psalm of praise.

"Praise the Lord, O my soul; all my inmost being, praise his holy name. Praise the Lord, O my soul, and forget not all his benefits," David sang (Ps. 103:1,2).

Satan hates praise, because it focuses our attention on God. But we can use it as a power-packed weapon to demolish strongholds, to tell the enemy he must back off, because God is our Father and He fights His children's battles.

The following are some Scripture prayers I use from time to time. I'm sure God will show you many others from His Word:

Father, in the name of Jesus, I come to Your throne to pre-

sent my children _____

before You. I stand in the gap between You and them and intercede on their behalf. You tell me to bind what is already bound in heaven and loose what is already loosed in heaven. I do that now in faith.

Therefore, Satan and your powers, rulers of darkness and spiritual forces of wickedness that have come against my children, I bind you in the mighty name of Jesus. Keep away from my children. I loose them to be all God has called them to be.

* * * * *

Father, I ask that You command Your angels concerning my

children, to guard them in all their ways (Ps. 91:11). You have promised that no harm will befall us and no disaster will come near our tent (Ps. 91:10). Thank You, Father. In Jesus' name, amen.

* * * * *

By the authority of Jesus Christ, my risen Savior and Lord, I bind you, Satan, and all your evil powers disturbing this situation today in the lives of my children. In the name of Jesus Christ, I command you to stop your maneuvers to hinder the Lord's will from being done (Matt. 18:18-20).

Ten

Praying in Trouble

"Arise, cry out in the night,…pour out your heart like water in the presence of the Lord. Lift up your hands to him for the lives of your children" (Lam. 2:19).

God wants access *to* us women so He can have access *through* us. Think about it. Women know what it is to labor and travail to bring forth physical life. Likewise, God will use yielded women to labor and travail to bring forth spiritual life—bringing our children out of darkness into the marvelous light of Jesus.

As praying mothers, we sometimes feel an urgency to travail in prayer for our children. We want them to be born-again and set free from bondages of cults, drugs, alcohol, or other worldly traps. When we give birth to our children in the natural, we often experience agony, pain, and weeping. Now the Spirit of God calls us to again be "in the pains of childbirth" (see Gal. 4:19).

"As a woman with child and about to give birth writhes and

cries out in her pain, so were we in your presence, O Lord," we read in Isaiah 26:17.

No one explained this dimension of prayer to me. My husband and I stumbled upon it when we hit a crisis with one of our children. We know now by experience what it means to fall on our faces with weeping, praying, and groaning. This is not something we can "work up." Rather it's the work of the Holy Spirit in us.

Even Jesus, while He lived on earth, offered up prayers and petitions with *"loud cries and tears" (Heb. 5:7)*.

Other scriptures speaking of weeping include Psalm 6:6,7, Nehemiah 1:4 and Lamentations 2:11,18,19.

But grab hold of this promise: *"Those who sow in tears will reap with songs of joy. He who goes out weeping, carrying seed to sow, will return with songs of joy, carrying sheaves with him" (Ps. 126:5,6)*. Yes, those who sow tears will reap joy.

For years, Dot's twenty-one-year-old daughter had loved her family and church. Suddenly she began going to wild parties with equally wild friends. Dot spent an entire day in travailing prayer—a great deal of it in a prone position on the floor—crying out for her daughter.

"I prayed in English. I prayed in tongues. I used spiritual warfare prayers from the Bible against Satan and his demonic forces. I groaned in my innermost being. Every once in a while I'd get up and pace the floor, praying aloud," Dot explained.

"I finally collapsed into an old rocker and was reading my Bible when Isaiah 54:13 was quickened to my heart. *'All your sons will be taught by the Lord, and great will be your children's peace.'"*

Wiping away her tears, Dot realized that "I had a relief from my prayer burden. I now had faith to trust God to accomplish what I asked. Somehow I knew the scripture would come true in my daughter's life, so I started thanking God that He would teach her and give her His peace. Six months later our daughter returned to the Lord and to our family. As an added bonus, He gave her new friends," she said.

"Was travailing prayer the turning point?" I asked.

"I believe so. Never have I felt such anguish of soul as I did that day, much like the day I delivered her after three days of labor pains. Only this time I felt I was wrestling for her very soul. Maybe I was," the mother admitted.

We must also be persistent in our prayers. Jesus told the story of a persistent man who did not give up until his friend got out of bed, opened the door, and gave him bread. He implied that we are to be likewise persistent in our asking. He further said: *"Keep on asking and it will be given you; keep on seeking and you will find; keep on knocking [reverently] and the door will be opened to you" (Matt 7:7 TAB).*

Let's examine the faith and persistent prayer of one of God's key prophets, Elijah. After Israel had suffered a three-and-a-half-year drought, the Lord told Elijah to present himself to King Ahab, and He would send rain.

Elijah confidently told the king, *"Go, eat and drink, for there is the sound of a heavy rain" (1 Kings 18:41).*

Notice Elijah believed that rain would come. God had promised it. But when he spoke those words, there was absolutely no visible evidence that rain was about to drench the sun-parched land. What did the prophet do? He climbed to the top of Mt. Carmel and crouched down on the ground with his head between his knees. This was the posture for a woman giving birth and meditating position for men in the Middle East. He then prayed earnestly seven times.

I think he was thanking God in advance that rain was on the way, though there certainly was no evidence yet. When the first tiny "sign" appeared, it was a mere cloud the size of a man's hand. A pint-size sign to some eyes, but not to Elijah. Before long the sky grew black with clouds, and a heavy rain came on. Old Ahab rode off to Jezreel in his chariot, but the power of the Lord came on Elijah and he ran ahead of Ahab all the way to Jezreel, twenty miles away.

Recently I relived this scene in my mind's eye as I stood on top of Mt. Carmel and looked out over the lush green plains leading to Jezreel. How I longed to have the depth of faith Elijah exhibited in this story recorded in 1 Kings 18.

I was encouraged later to read in James 5:17,18 that Elijah was a human with a nature like ours, not some exalted personage. As an ordinary human being, he offered his earnest prayers in faith.

How can we apply the lesson of Elijah's prayer time to our lives? Sometimes the Lord lets us know that our children are coming out of a crisis situation. It is time now to believe God, stand on His Word, and thank Him in advance for answered prayer. In the meantime, we pray persistently, sometimes in travail, letting the Holy Spirit in us groan with words that cannot even be expressed.

Sally, a mother who stood with an Elijah-like faith, shared about a trying period in her son's life.

"When my son Todd turned sixteen, it seemed I'd lost touch with him. He was uptight and silent a lot. Simply in a shell. Worst of all, there was evidence he'd cut himself off from God, too. I watched powerlessly as other boys exerted more influence over him that we did at home. My only recourse was prayer.

"Then late one afternoon I was walking the beach alone, talking to the Lord about him. After more than an hour, I reached down and picked up a small brown-and-white shell that was being tossed about helplessly by giant waves. When I did, I had an inner awareness that God was saying, 'This shell had much potential for growth. So does your son. Just trust Me to polish and perfect him.'"

Sally took her "promise shell" home, washed it in bleach, and set it on her kitchen-window ledge. Often she'd pick it up, lift it high in the air, and breathe a triumphant prayer, "Lord, You promised."

Todd drifted further and further into open rebellion. One afternoon he stormed out of the house screaming at his mother, "I can't be the kind of Christian you want me to be!" then disappeared until the wee hours of the morning. As the months crept by, he continued to get into all kinds of teenage mischief. Sally watched sadly but continued her travailing for him.

When Todd went away to college, there was still no sign of repentance or change for the better. Four years had elapsed since Sally had received her promise on the beach. Then one night she felt an urgency to write to her son about her special "promise shell," ending her letter with a paraphrase of the scripture she'd clung to: *I've held unswervingly to the hope I profess, for He who promised is faithful"* (see Heb. 10:23).

A short time later Todd wrote back.

"Mom, your letter made me so happy I almost cried. You don't know this, but Tuesday, the night you wrote the letter, Mom, I went into the city to hear a Christian band perform. I'd really been in the pit. But I gave it all to God. I feel great. I know it won't be easy, but we'll make it this time. I appreciate now all that you and Dad have done for me. Thanks. And thank God for His 'promise shell.'"

If we ask Him, God will often give us special assurance for our children. It may come from a Scripture verse, or as in Sally's case, from something personal God whispers to our spirits. When it comes, we can stand on that word with sure faith. Until we see His promise actually fulfilled, we will have some hours of persistent prayer in store, but we must never give up. God is faithful.

Evangelist Dave Wilkerson observes, "In recent months the

Holy Spirit has been awakening husbands, wives, and grand-parents and calling believers back to a deeper walk in the Spirit. There is a cleansing going on everywhere, with the Spirit brooding over homes, bringing back tears of repentance and growing hunger for reality."

Never before have I heard the depth of wailing, travailing prayer as that offered at the Western Wall in Jerusalem. Here at the only remains of the wall that once surrounded the temples built in Solomon's and Herod's times, pilgrims—Jews and Christians alike—from around the world come to pray. Twenty-four hours a day people stand at the wall praying, many weeping openly.

When I was there one cold February Sunday, a woman next to me sobbed uncontrollably as she pressed her body against the wall. Every once in a while she'd push another slip of paper with a loved one's name written on it into a crack in the wall and wail louder. Though she was a stranger, I felt a kinship with her. I joined my prayers with hers. "Lord, it's Your will to save. Give her family repentant hearts," I said softly as she continued her travailing. We were two mothers from opposite sides of the globe praying for our families.

Intercession has been called "God's birthing process." Mothers who have experienced travailing prayer can say, "Amen."

Eleven

Praying for Our Wayward Children

"He will even deliver the one [for whom you intercede] who is not innocent; yes, he will be delivered through the cleanness of your hands" (Job 22:30 TAB).

The snow was still a foot deep following a freak three-day winter storm. As my husband drove cautiously down the icy pavement, I spied a little lost black lamb not far from the roadside, bogged down helplessly in the white blanket. "Look, look!" I shouted a few minutes later as a farmer stomped his way over to the tiny black ball of wool, swooshed him up in his arms, and headed toward the nearby farmhouse to return him safely to his fold.

My sagging spirits lifted. We had just spent three days cooped indoors praying about a troublesome situation in the life of one of our precious "lambs." God was reminding me once again that Jesus, the Good Shepherd, was out looking for His sheep.

And He's out looking for yours, too.

If you have a wayward child, take hope. Picture that one restored to wholeness, singing praises to Jesus. Hold tightly to that image. Then read Luke 15—the "lost and found" chapter. You, too, will find reason to rejoice.

This passage has encouraged many downhearted parents. For one thing, it shows us that the Good Shepherd leaves the ninety-nine sheep to go hunting for the lost one. He finds it, heaves it over His shoulder, and brings it back safely. Calling His friends, He says, *"Rejoice with me; I have found my lost sheep" (Luke 15:6)*.

One of the most heartwarming examples of our time has been the restoration of Franklin, son of evangelist Billy Graham. Now an ordained minister serving in missions, Franklin was once a young rebel.

One night while praying for her "lost lamb," as his mother called him, she slipped to her knees to commit Franklin once again to the Lord. She realized she must first "commit what was left of me to God." She did this, then sought God's response. "He impressed me, 'You take care of the possible and trust Me for the impossible.'" On the day of Franklin's ordination, his mother shared her story and added, "Today you are seeing the impossible."[1]

"But that was Billy Graham's son," we might say. "What about ordinary people with wayward children?"

I know another mother who never quit praying for her daughter Carolyn, who by the age of eighteen had become a popular television model. Disillusioned, the girl turned to alcohol, drugs, and sex to find fulfillment. Although she had been raised in the church, she became a drug pusher to support her habits. She turned her back on everything she'd learned, deliberately running from God.

Then one night when she was thirty-nine and completely

disgusted with what she had become, Carolyn knelt beside her bed and cried three little words, "God help me!"

"I fell on my knees a sinner and stood up knowing Jesus was my Savior and Lord," she relates. "I ran down to the cocktail lounge where I was part-owner and told everyone in there about Jesus. I never again had a desire to touch alcohol or drugs. In fact, shortly afterward I left the lounge to my partner and moved away to start life over again. My mother had prayed for me for twenty years and never given up hope. I know it was her prayers that brought me through to repentance," she admits now.

For three years I've watched Carolyn as she's brought one after another to the Lord, many of them down-and-outers like she once was.

Through our prayers, mothers, the Shepherd is out wooing our lambs back to the fold—lambs like Franklin and Carolyn. Our part is to pray with confidence that our unsaved children will be receptive when the Shepherd comes to them.

As we read on in Luke 15, we see the story of the Prodigal Son. I call him the "give-me son," because he demanded his inheritance before it was due him. He may have added, "Dad, you can't die soon enough for me. Give me what's mine so I can get out of this dull place."

No amount of pleading, bargaining, or threatening would have changed that son's mind. Some of us know what that feels like. We've been wounded by our children. But can we, like the father of the Prodigal Son, forgive? Can we believe that regardless of the circumstances, some day we will walk out in our front yards and see our repentant sons or daughters coming home?

Notice how badly that son "blew it." He went to a distant country and spent his entire inheritance on reckless living. When famine hit the land, he would have gladly eaten the pods the hogs were eating, but no one gave him anything. He knew his father's hired servants had it better than he did. So he came to his senses and headed home, willing to be just a servant.

While the son was still a long way off, his father saw him coming. This convinces me that the father believed that someday he'd be back. He looked for him expectantly every day. When the father spied his wayward son, he was so filled with compassion, he ran to meet him, threw his arms around him and kissed him over and over again. Imagine smothering a stinking, dirty boy straight from the pig pen with love, even before he knew he had a repentant heart. But that's what this loving parent did. What a party he threw. The son which was lost was found, restored. What rejoicing!

When Jane's son Jeff became addicted to alcohol and drugs as a young teenager, she drew closer to the Lord. Often she lay on her bedroom floor interceding for him in every possible way she could find in the Bible. At other times she'd go into his bedroom and pray against all attacks the enemy staged against Jeff. For months she interceded while Jeff rode off with a Hell's Angels' motorcycle gang. She prayed two significant prayers: "God, I free You to do anything You have to do to bring forth a man of God in my son." Then she prayed, "God, come and establish Your throne in Jeff's life."

"After praying for months, one day I knew my warfare was over," Jane says. "The burden lifted, although there was no significant change in Jeff. I had that inner knowing that I could stop my deep intercession. For awhile things got worse. Six months later, Jeff got some 'angel dust' and came close to losing his sanity.

"In desperation he cried, 'God show me the way out,'" Jane continued. "His prayer was answered through a Christian on his job who helped him find his way to the Lord. Jeff was soon delivered of cigarettes, alcohol, and drugs. Today he has an ongoing relationship with the Lord and preaches, sings, and plays the piano at a little mission on skid row. God has done a powerful restoration in this rebel boy. Don't ever doubt the power of your prayers as a warring mother," Jane says.

If there was ever a rebel it was Aurelius Augustinus, better known today as St. Augustine of Italy. Although his mother Monica had prayed for him daily since he'd been a young boy, Augustine went his own way and explored various philosophies. He maintained a mistress for over fifteen years who bore him an illegitimate child.

Yet strong-minded, practical Monica was determined her wayward son would become a Christian. Once she even appealed to an African bishop to talk to Augustine about his soul. The bishop refused but comforted the heartbroken mother with words that held high promise: "Only pray to the Lord on his behalf. It is impossible for the son of such tears to perish."

And pray she did.

One day Augustine picked up a Bible and read Romans 13. Suddenly, all his doubts and arguments against Christianity fled. He accepted Jesus. When he told his mother, she almost shouted, "Praise God who is able to do above that which we ask or think!" Nine days later, her lifelong prayers answered, Monica passed away.

For the next forty-four years, Augustine read and interpreted the Scriptures. As Bishop of Hippo he was one of the most influential men of his time. He died in 430 A.D., leaving writings that brought spiritual illumination to thousands through the centuries.[2]

My friend Barbara had a rebel son, too. After she became a Christian, she sought the Lord about him. One day when she was reading the second chapter of Joel, this verse pierced her heart: *"'Even now,' declares the Lord, 'return to me with all your heart, with fasting and weeping and mourning'" (v. 12).*

Through that verse, God shone a spotlight on her heart, revealing her bitterness, anger, and unforgiveness. So she repented with fasting, weeping, and prayer. She also asked God to change her.

Then she happily read the verse in the second chapter of Joel in which God said He would repay her for the years the locusts had eaten (v. 25).

"Even though I hadn't been the right parent my son needed in his growing-up years, God had now forgiven me and placed a promise in my heart," she recently told me. "I believed that He would restore the years the stripping, evil 'locusts' had eaten from my life and that my son would accept the Lord."

For Barbara, that was a big leap of faith. You see, for some years her son had been in prison. Today he is still in prison, but at the age of twenty-nine, he accepted Jesus.

Barbara is one of the most joyous Christian mothers I've ever known. What's more, she's a strong intercessor for her state's prison system. She prays for the inmates, guards, superintendent, and chaplains. Many mothers might be so devastated at having a son in prison that they'd never think to intercede for others there, but not Barbara. Out of a bad situation, God has brought forth good.

Yes, she believes that some day her son will physically return home. But the Lord has already been faithful to His promise. The Good Shepherd found her lost lamb, even behind bars.

Twelve

Praying in Faith

"Train a child in the way he should go, and when he is old he will not turn from it" (Prov. 22:6).

"Your son is on drugs. I'm sorry but I told Richard if he didn't confess to you, I'd have to tell you myself." Their best friend dropped this devastating bomb on Pastor Peter Lord and his wife Johnnie. In their extremity, they sought God.

Pastor Lord wisely recognized that mothers often are more sensitive to the Lord's leading regarding their children than fathers, so he suggested that his wife Johnnie go into seclusion to fast, pray, and seek guidance from God about their oldest son. Of course, while Johnnie was away, Peter also was in deep intercession.

Reeling from this terrible blow, Johnnie Lord cried and cried before the Lord on behalf of Richard.

On the third morning of her fast, God quickened two Bible verses to her heart: The first was, *"Now to him who is able to do immeasurably more than all we ask or imagine" (Eph. 3:20).*

The second was likewise powerful: *"The Lord will fulfill his purpose for me" (Ps. 138:8).*

Rejoicing, she asked, "Lord, what purpose do You have for Richard's life?"

"Very clearly, the Lord assured me He was going to use Richard in His redemptive plan for others," she remembers.

When she got home, Johnnie told her husband, "Richard might as well give up his bad habits and new friends, because God is going to use him in His work."

Despite her optimism, Richard went from bad to worse.

Pastor Lord likewise prayed, but he tried to bargain with God.

"God, do anything You have to do to get Richard's attention—anything, but don't let him go to jail."

"Why can't he go to jail?"

"Well, You know, Lord, newspapers print sensational stories. It wouldn't look good for Your kingdom to have headlines telling everyone the pastor's son is in jail on drug charges."

When the Lord showed him his pride, Peter obediently confessed it as sin and prayed again, "Okay, do anything to bring Richard back to You, Lord. Anything."

A few days later the inevitable happened. Richard was jailed in another city. When his parents visited him, they took him his mail. Inside was his income-tax return, so with that money he paid his own bail bond.

Did his jail experience jolt him back on course? No. But his mother continued to pray, repeatedly reminding the Lord that Richard had been trained in the ways of the Lord. She held on to God's promises to her during her solitary time of fasting.

She also thanked the Lord for Richard's commendable qualities—his being voted the most popular boy in his senior class and receiving a small college scholarship.

The weeks crept into months with no sign of improvement

as Richard continued his rebellious life-style.

Then one day unexpectedly, Richard moved home. He caught up on his sleep, devoured nourishing meals, and attended church regularly—a condition his Dad made to him when he came home.

One Friday night Richard quietly encountered Jesus and surrendered his heart to Him. In the meantime, his drug charges were miraculously dropped.

Soon afterward, Richard enrolled in a Christian college and later graduated from seminary. Now in his first church as pastor, he has helped free many young people involved in drug-and-alcohol abuse by introducing them to Jesus and the enabling power of the Holy Spirit.

Yes, God did "immeasurably more than all" his mother could ask or think! What would have happened if those parents' prayers had not been answered as quickly as they were? Knowing Peter and Johnnie Lord as I do, I can safely say they would still be standing on their promises from God with much faith.

If we've raised children in our Christian homes, then watched them turn away from God, Johnnie Lord offers an encouraging word: "Regardless of how bad the situation looks to you, thank God He's at work in your child, bringing him back on course. Never give up hope," she says.

Even in our panic, we must not forget that God's Word tells us that if we have trained our children in the way they should go, when they are old they will not turn from it.

Meanwhile, in our waiting times, we can affirm with Paul: *"We live by faith, not by sight" (2 Cor. 5:7).*

Thirteen

Praying for Our Godly Children

"We have not stopped praying for you and asking God to fill you with the knowledge of his will through all spiritual wisdom and understanding" (Col. 1:9).

How should you pray for "good children"? a mother asks. "They are already living for the Lord, and they don't cause anyone any trouble. Shouldn't we pray more for unbelievers and leave the young people who are already serving God to the care of the Holy Spirit?"

Paul called the Colossians *"faithful brothers in Christ" (Col. 1:2).* Even though he recognized them as true believers, he saw they still had a need for prayer, and so he said he had not stopped praying for them.

Yes, good children—those who are walking with the Lord— need a mother's prayers just as much as the renegades do. The enemy is not happy that these children are walking with the Lord,

74

and he will do everything in his power to try to waylay them. He will tempt them, discourage them, and cause others to speak ill of them. He might even cause them to be so busy *doing* for the Lord that they forget that it is more important to *be* what God wants them to be. Since Satan is crafty and wily, "good kids" need the hedge of protection that prayer provides just as much as kids outside of God's household.

Susanna, the mother of John and Charles Wesley, the great preacher and hymn writer respectively, taught them the alphabet while they were very young children. Shortly afterward they began to read the Bible.

Susanna Wesley was a woman of action, a strict but fair disciplinarian, and a woman of prayer. It is reported that she prayed daily with John and Charles and with each of her other living children (she had nineteen, not all of whom survived). She knew the importance of consistent daily prayer in the lives of her godly children. Perhaps it is no wonder that two of her sons accomplished so much in the kingdom of God.

A modern-day mother, Laura, tells why she prays for her children. "All of mine need daily help to walk faithfully with the Lord. Godly children, just like children who are not so godly, are also beset with temptations. I ask God to protect them from all harm because the enemy will work to discourage them. I pray that they will have an increased concept of who they are in Jesus. And I pray for the fruit of the Holy Spirit to be evidenced in their lives. I pray daily a portion of the Lord's prayer for mine: *'Lead (them) not into temptation, but deliver (them) from the evil one' (Matt. 6:13)."*

Praying for those we love to be kept from temptation is not a new idea. Jesus prayed for Peter about this very matter:

"Simon, Simon, Satan has asked to sift you as wheat. But I have prayed for you, Simon, that your faith may not fail."

To which Simon Peter replied, *"Lord, I am ready to go with you to prison and to death" (Luke 22:31-33).* No doubt, Peter truly meant what he was saying at the moment. But Jesus knew that just ahead was a fierce temptation to sin by denying Him. He knew that Peter was going to fail. Rather than being angry with him, He simply prayed and then added this instruction, *"And when you have turned back, strengthen your brothers" (v. 32).*

Jesus prayed not only for Peter, but for all His disciples. In His great prayer in which He committed His followers to God's keeping, He prays:

"I have revealed you to those whom you gave me out of the world. They were yours; you gave them to me and they have obeyed your word....For I gave them the words you gave me and they accepted them....I pray for them. I am not praying for the world, but for those you have given me, for they are yours....Protect them by the power of your name—the name you gave me—so that they may be one as we are one" (John 17:6,8,9,11).

If Jesus prayed this way for His spiritual children, then we as parents should pray even more for our believing children that they will be protected by the power of Jesus' name. We can pray, "Dear Lord, I bring my children to you. They have heard the Word of God which I have taught them, and they have believed. Now keep them, protect them by the power of Your name, Lord Jesus Christ. Don't let the Evil One steal away the teaching they have received, but rather let it grow in them. Make them mighty men and women of God to Your honor and glory."

Beth's four married daughters and their husbands and children all love and serve the Lord. Every day she prays for them individually by name:

1. That they not be deceived
2. That they not walk in error
3. That they will be counted worthy to stand before the Lord

at His coming.

The apostle Paul also prayed for those under his care. First he commends their faithfulness to God, *"To the saints in Ephesus, the faithful in Christ Jesus" (Eph. 1:1).* These were strong believers. Then he tells them how he prays for them:

"For this reason, ever since I heard about your faith in the Lord Jesus and your love for all the saints, I have not stopped giving thanks for you, remembering you in my prayers" (Eph. 1:15,16).

And what was it that Paul prayed for these believing saints? *"I keep asking that the God of our Lord Jesus Christ, the glorious Father, may give you the Spirit of wisdom and revelation, so that you may know him better" (Eph. 1:17).*

What a wonderful thing to pray for our believing children that God would give them the "Spirit of wisdom and revelation" in order that they would know Him better. What more could we parents ask than for our children to come to know God better? What higher goal for children to attain to than wisdom and revelation? We need people in our world with wisdom who know what needs to be done and how God wants it done.

Then Paul went on: *"I pray also that the eyes of your heart may be enlightened in order that you may know the hope to which he has called you, the riches of his glorious inheritance in the saints, and his incomparably great power for us who believe" (Eph. 1:18,19).*

This is a valid prayer for Christian parents to use. In a time when there seems to be so little hope, we need to pray that our children may know the hope to which they have been called. They need to see that this life is not all there is, that they already are rich because of what they are to inherit. They are already heirs and heiresses in the kingdom of God.

And then let's talk about this "incomparably great power" that Paul mentions. What is it that is promised to those who believe?

"That power is like the working of his mighty strength, which he exerted in Christ when he raised him from the dead and seated him at his right hand in the heavenly realms, far above all rule and authority, power and dominion, and every title that can be given, not only in the present age but also in the one to come" *(Eph. 1:19-21).*

Do we understand that Paul is asking for the believers to have the same kind of power in their lives as the power that raised Christ from the dead, the same power that seated Him at God's right hand, the same power that has given Jesus Christ all dominion and authority? That's what Paul is asking for his beloved Ephesian children, and that's what we parents can ask for our children who are already followers of Jesus Christ.

Our children can become powerhouses to change the world. Among them will be great evangelists, preachers, teachers, and missionaries who will help to bring salvation to our world. Some will have the gift of faith to pray for the sick and see them healed. Some will have gifts of administration to bring order and progress to the church. Others will be great musicians whose songs will melt hard, unbelieving hearts. Some will be writers and publishers of Christian materials. Still others will be politicians who will change the face of politics and turn their nations toward God.

There is no limit to what can be accomplished by these godly young people who are empowered by the Holy Spirit and are supported by the prayers of believing parents. God is looking for people through whom He can change the world. He may want to use our sons or daughters.

Let's pray that our children will influence an ungodly world. Pray that they will reveal Christ to their fellow students and teachers in school. Pray that they will be both "salt" and "light" to the world in which they move. Jesus said, *"Let your light shine before men, that they may see your good deeds and praise your Father in heaven" (Matt. 5:16).* Only God knows what will happen if we Christian parents truly pray for our children to become forces for righteousness in their schools and places of work.

One young mother's last act before sending her two children out the door to school was to pray for them. She prayed that their school work would go well, that they would have a good day with their classmates, that God would help their teachers, and that their lives would be witnesses for Jesus Christ.

This daily ritual by the front door became such an important part of their lives that if she forgot, one or the other would say, "Mom, aren't you going to pray for us today?" One day a child said, "Mom, pray for my teacher; her husband is dying." Sometimes their requests were for friends who had sinned or were having problems at home. Because of all the prayers, these young people had an influence for God in their secular schools all their growing-up years. They had an awareness that they were ambassadors for Christ in a sinful world. It influenced the way they lived and acted.

Now one of them is a college student living at home and things have not changed too much. When there is a speech to give, a difficult exam ahead, or a marathon session to get a term paper done, it is still, "Mom, can you pray for me?"

Let's pray that our children will be examples not only to a sinful world, but to the believing world as well. Paul had much to say about this to his spiritual son Timothy. It would be well for a parent to read through both of the books of Timothy to see the kind of instruction and prayer Paul gave the young man.

On one occasion he advised him, *"Don't let anyone look down on you because you are young, but set an example for the believers in speech, in life, in love, in faith and in purity' (1 Tim. 4:12).*

Paul realized the importance of the young believer's example on others who believe. Young people need to be aware that they do not live for themselves. Each young person is setting an example for some younger person who looks up to him with trust. The exuberance of youth encourages older saints to know that the kingdom of God rests in good hands and is going to continue.

Young people who are taught to pray know how to pray. Some of them become prayer warriors, committing large blocks of time to prayer.

Interestingly enough, most of the great revivals of the past have come about when young people, often college-aged students, have devoted themselves to prayer.

In fact, the great move of the Holy Spirit in this century began in Topeka, Kansas, when a group of Bible-school students prayed in three-hour shifts around the clock. Day and night, prayer ascended to God from the fervent hearts of these young people. And on the first day of 1901, God poured out His Spirit on the praying students.

For the next three days young people prayed, praised, gave thanks, and worshipped God without taking a break. From there the revival spread to neighboring cities and towns, then to neighboring states and finally to Azusa, California, where in a former Methodist church building believers began to meet and pray. That revival lasted three years, going on night and day without a break.

People from all over the world visited that revival. Many were baptized in the Holy Spirit. Hundreds were converted. From there the Pentecostal revival spread around the world.

Young people who are committed to God can have a powerful effect on the world through prayer and the examples of their lives.

Paul has another word of admonition to Timothy that we can pray for our young people. He says, *"Do not neglect your gift, which was given you through a prophetic message when the body of elders laid their hands on you" (1 Tim. 4:14).*

He undoubtedly is referring to an event that happened at the time of Timothy's ordination. But to each believer God gives gifts. Each of our children is gifted by God to do something in a certain way that no other person on earth can do. Pray that God will bring the gift or gifts to the forefront of his life. Pray that he will be encouraged to stir up the gifts God has given him so he will do something with them.

Satan would like to discourage our children from using their gifts and abilities for God. He makes sure that there are many calls from the world and opportunities for them to use their talents there rather than in service to Christ. Let's pray that our children will dedicate their abilities to God.

Then let's pray for the lifework of our children, that God will lead them into the places He wants them to be. And while we are at it, we should pray for ourselves and our spouses as well. What would we do if God called our children into service halfway around the world? Before we answer too quickly, think what that would mean. How often would we get to see our grandchildren? What kind of unsanitary, unsafe situations would our young people live in—without complaint from us? What about our lonely old age when they could only visit us every three or four years?

Jesus said, *"Ask the Lord of the harvest, therefore, to send out workers into his harvest field" (Matt. 9:38).* That's not too hard to do until we realize that the workers He may want to send are our own children.

There is a dying, lost world to reach, and no one knows how long we have to reach it. Let's pray that God will use our godly young people in that harvest field, whether at home or abroad, whether in full-time ministry or in the marketplace of our country. God will use anyone He finds who is willing, no matter what his occupation is.

One mother with tears in her eyes told her pastor's wife, "To think that I prayed and gave my child to God's keeping, and now He's called her to be a missionary. It is more than I could have asked for."

There was no sorrow in this mother's heart, only great joy that God had chosen her child for His special call and purposes.

Another man, a middle-age missionary, had just learned that his mother was seriously ill. He was concerned that she might die. "If I lose my mother, who will pray for me?" he said. "Other people tell me that they pray for me, but I don't know if they really do. She is the only person on earth I can truly count on to stand with me in prayer."

Then too we must not forget to pray for our children's spouses. Even if they are very young, it is not too soon to begin praying for those persons who will one day be in our families. Billy Graham and his wife began praying for their children's mates when the children were very young, and they have encouraged others to do the same.

Let's pray for the spiritual lives of those mates and that our children will be willing to wait for God's choices and not settle for second best. We should pray that in God's time and way, they will come together. Let's pray that their lives together will be examples of Christ and His bride to the church and that together they may win souls to Christ and further serve the kingdom of God.

If we see the need for praying for our godly children and yet find it hard to pray, we can do as we've mentioned before. We can bring the Word of God to the Lord and make it our own. By doing this, we are saying, "Yes, Lord" to the passages written in His Word.

Several mothers I know use Isaiah 11:2 as a prayer-pattern, although they recognize it was initially speaking of the coming

Messiah:

"Father, I pray that the Spirit of the Lord will rest on

_____, the Spirit of wisdom

and of understanding, the Spirit of counsel and of power, the Spirit of knowledge and of the fear of the Lord."

Still other mothers find Paul's prayer helpful:

"I pray that God will fill _____with the knowledge of His will through all spiritual wisdom and

understanding, that _____may live a life

worthy of the Lord and may please Him in every way, bearing fruit in every good work, growing in the knowledge of God, being strengthened with all power according to His glorious

might so that _____may have great

endurance and patience, and joyfully share in the inheritance of the saints" (Col. 1:9-12).

Wayward or godly, our children benefit by our "standing in the gap" for them in prayer.

Fourteen

Praying for Our Married Children

"But as for me and my household, we will serve the Lord" (Josh. 24:15).

A mother's prayers for her married children naturally include their spouses too—prayers for right career choices, for fellowship with believers, for godly homes, for God's direction, guidance, and wisdom in every endeavor.

Laura prayed for many years that her daughter's husband would have a closer relationship with the Lord. In the meantime, she loved and accepted him as he was. As the years went on, she saw some encouraging signs. Once when doctors believed his mom had lung cancer, he asked Laura to pray. When the tissue sample turned out to be benign, he phoned Laura with the news, "The doctor said Mom's lung tissue looked like raw beefsteak pounded with a mallet and should have been cancerous. But we know how she was healed, don't we?"

Laura shared another powerful testimony with me: "My grandmother York prayed for each of her six children, their spouses, children, and grandchildren by name every day," she said. "She kept up with what was happening to them so she could pray specifically. Now twenty-five years after her death, all her descendants are Christians."

That should encourage all of us mothers not to grow fainthearted in our praying.

Let's believe that it is God's will for our children's spouses to be saved, and surrender them to the Lord. We must be assured that He will draw them to Himself because we have entrusted them to Him. Again, we can leave up to God the time and the way He works in their lives.

"We have to accept our in-law-children as they are and be emotional and spiritual supports," one mother-in-law wrote.

Tears filled Esther's pale blue eyes as she told me about her beautiful daughter Diane who became a paraplegic as the result of an automobile accident when she was in her early twenties.

"After that she became rebellious and angry at us and God," Esther said. "During this period, she married a non-Christian. My heart was broken. What had happened to all those prayers I'd prayed for her? I wondered.

"Today she and her husband have a darling little girl—a precious miracle of God. As I was praying the other morning, the Lord impressed on me that since my son-in-law Tim had lost both his parents, I was to stand in the gap for him. I believe he will soon accept Jesus as Savior and Lord and be the Christian husband I prayed for Diane to have years ago," Esther continued.

"Since I've trained Diane in the ways of the Lord, I have His promise that when she is old, she will not depart from them. So I can stand in faith for her and Tim. Already I see a softening, a slight responding," Esther told me with a smile as she dug into her wallet for a photo of her little granddaughter.

Even during turbulent times, we can praise God for the future fulfillment of His promises for all those in our households.

Our daughters Quinett and Sherry are praying that God will give them husbands like David of old who was *"a brave man and a warrior,"* who spoke well and was fine-looking and the Lord was with him (1 Sam. 16:18).

One day our son Keith told his fiancee, "You are a jewel, a real treasure. My mom prayed for my future wife for years. She didn't know your name, but she was covering you with prayer."

A lump the size of a log jammed in my throat when Keith told me about it. I remembered during his rebellious years when I had wondered if he knew or cared that I was praying for him and for his future. Today he is a graphic artist for a top Christian magazine and involved in a new but growing church. His future bride hopes to use her singing abilities for the Lord, too.

When we comforted one of our daughters whose engagement was broken, we marveled at her ability to go on with God and not look back. Within a couple of weeks, she sat down and scribbled out a prayer asking the Lord to bring His special man into her life in His timing and way.

In the meantime, her dad and I returned wedding gifts, sent out announcements that the wedding was off, and tried to keep level heads about it all. With God's help we made it through yet another family crisis because He is teaching us how to pray for our children.

Fifteen

Praying for Our
Handicapped Children

"Anyone who will not receive the kingdom of God like a little child will never enter it" (Mark 10:15).

"You are a special mom if without bitterness or rebellion you can see your handicapped child as God's special gift to you," says the mother of a child with cerebral palsy.

My friend Bonnie has three active, healthy children and a four-year-old son Adam who has this crippling disease. She readily shares some ways she prays for Adam:

1. "I pray that other children will accept my child and will try to be his friend, though he is different.

2. "For myself, our children, and our enlarged family, I pray for wisdom and unending patience.

3. "For my handicapped son, I pray that his life will glorify God on earth by completing the work God has given him to do (John 17:4). I pray for Adam's potential to be maximized and

the purpose for his life to be fully realized as it touches others.

4. "Yes, I pray for his healing, and I wait."

I'm sure God has placed similar prayers in the hearts of thousands of other mothers who like Bonnie have a special child to love, care for, and nurture in prayer.

I rejoiced with Bonnie when a nursery school teacher who had worked with Adam for a year wrote her about her own heart change.

She said, "I took a good look at Adam and knew there was something missing in my teaching. I decided the only way to become like him was to let the Lord take over my life. Jesus said that unless we become as little children, we shall not enter heaven. Adam is a gift from God with a special purpose on this earth. Through him the Lord showed me the way to Jesus."

A little child had led her to the Master.

Brenda and George Waller have a handsome fourteen-year-old son Ben who sits in church quietly beside them. What's so unusual is that Ben is both autistic and retarded. But bathed in his parents' continual prayers, he is functioning without medication.

"Why me?" Brenda asked when the doctors told her Ben not only had a cleft palate but was retarded and autistic. "Was it because He could trust us with such a little treasure? I only know I pressed closer and closer to the Lord after Ben came into our lives. At first I refused to accept his limitations. I told myself he was just a slow learner. As time passed, I had to accept the doctor's diagnosis, but I didn't have to accept all the negative things he told me to expect throughout his life. I determined we would have as normal a family life as possible—I vowed that to my husband and the other children. With God's help, I think we've done that."

Ben is on no medication to control hyperactivity or any other aspects of his condition. Since he refuses to take medication when he is sick, his parents have to depend on God to heal him. "God seems to answer our prayers for Ben quicker than our other prayers. At night we often pray over him while he sleeps, asking the Lord to reach down and touch him in every area of his life, including his physical body," Brenda said.

Those who have known Ben over the years agree that he has shown marked improvement. His parents thank the Lord for that, and they trust that Ben will someday be restored in mind and body.

Charlotte, whose husband lay in a coma for thirteen years and only recently died, has a forty-five-year-old retarded daughter. Emily lives four hundred miles away from her mother with the supervisor of the day-care center where she is employed. Charlotte thanks God daily for providing for Emily's needs.

"The Lord has been gracious in sending people who now accept Emily and give her the opportunity to be as productive and well-adjusted as she is," Charlotte said. "She loves working with the babies and toddlers in the center. She rocks them, changes their diapers, sings to them, and says their prayers with them. What's more, she makes a salary that lets her pay room and board to the family she lives with. She catches the bus to work and walks to a little church down the street on Sunday," Charlotte explained.

The second of four children, Emily was exposed to prayers and Bible reading at home just as the others were. Then twelve years ago, according to her mother, Emily cried out to God for the Holy Spirit to fill her and meet her needs.

"She realized she was severely rejected by other people—even by those in the church we attended in our tiny town—but she knew Jesus wouldn't reject her. In this hard circumstance, God met her need. She's closer to the Lord than my other children, and she never misses an opportunity to share what Jesus has done for her. She says she talks to Jesus about everything and He tells her what to do. It's beautiful to watch her childlike faith, her devotion to the Lord," that mother told me, handing me the latest picture of Emily sporting a chic new haircut and a broad smile.

"Accepting a child like Emily is, I think, the first step to wholeness for a mother with a handicapped child," Charlotte continued. "To pray for that child and watch God answer prayers in the little nitty-gritty areas of her life is an awesome and humbling experience. Since God has provided for her physical needs, I continue to pray He will fill her spiritual hunger and let her little light be a faithful one for Him. I thank Him for the level of love we've come to know through Emily and what she's taught our family. She's been a blessing. So I ask God to continue to bless her," Charlotte said.

Recently when Mark, one of my children's twenty-one-year-old friends, died from a disease that had plagued him since birth, I wrote his mom a note. Her response was one I treasure: "Thank you for remembering. Somehow Mark's life has made his death easier for us. He wasn't bitter, had no quarrel with God, and didn't feel sorry for himself. He seemed to see himself as one whom God richly blessed. And so he was. And so are we all."

My prayer partner Carol lost a fourteen-year-old son before I knew her. She told me that she had called every pastor in her small community and asked them to announce Hal's death on Sunday from their pulpits with a message: "Tell your people nothing we gave Hal—an education, material things, even love—nothing counted except that he knew Jesus and has eternal life."

Whenever she prays for a need for someone close to her, Carol asks God to take that prayer and use it for others with similar needs—perhaps grieving or distraught mothers.

When a child is lost in death, it helps to remember that God is our partner in grief. Jesus has already gone through His sufferings with death and waits to minister to our pain.

Almost all of us know a mother of a child with an abnormality who needs our undergirding prayers and support. Our fourteen-year-old niece Karen is not yet able to do basics such as dress herself, use the potty, even talk. How I admire and take courage from her mom who has a depth of compassion I've not personally experienced.

A promising scripture for all of us mothers—especially for moms like Karen's is this: *"I know whom I have believed, and am convinced that he is able to guard what I have entrusted to him for that day" (2 Tim. 1:12).*

Sixteen

Praying for the Unborn

"The angel said to him, Do not be afraid, Zechariah, because your petition was heard, and your wife Elizabeth will bear you a son....He will be great and distinguished in the sight of the Lord...and he will be filled with and controlled by the Holy Spirit, even in and from his mother's womb" (Luke 1:13,15 TAB).

The above passage refers to John the Baptist, son of Zechariah and Elizabeth, born to them in their old age. As forerunner of the Messiah, he was filled with the Holy Spirit in his mother's womb.

In response to this scripture Dr. Francis MacNutt and his wife Judith began a deliberate prayer program for their first child from the moment they knew she had been conceived. The MacNutts are but one of a growing number of Christian couples who believe

92

that parents' spiritual conditions affect the unborn. They have ample reason to believe this since extensive research verifies the effect of parents' attitudes on their unborn.

In his book *The Secret Life of the Unborn Child,* Thomas Verny, M.D., reports that clinical studies show that a baby in the womb hears, tastes, feels, and learns. What he experiences begins to shape his attitudes and expectations about himself. For example, in tests unborn babies responded calmly to the gentle music of Mozart but reacted with violent motion to performances of Beethoven and rock music. A baby in the womb, he says, learns to recognize his parents' voices, is comforted by soothing tones, and is upset, fearful, and jumpy when parents quarrel.[1]

The MacNutts prayed twice a day accompanied with the laying-on-of-hands on the mother, until their child was born.

Dr. MacNutt writes in a magazine article, "Our prayers were spoken out loud, but were simple. We were not trying to communicate with the child except through our attitudes, but we were communicating with God in the child's presence."

Sometimes they prayed for themselves—to be the kind of parents they should be for the child: "Our Father, deliver us from the Evil One. Deliver us from all sickness, from all accidents and harm of every kind. Prepare us to be the kind of parents we should be for this little one."

At other times they prayed specifically for the baby: "Fill this child with Your presence and Your life. Let this child be especially beloved by You. Watch over Your own child. Fill it with health and happiness and the great desire to be born, a great love for life, an excitement for things spiritual."

They deliberately did not pray for any preference for the child's sex, not wanting their child to later feel rejection due to their projections of sexual favor.[2]

Harvey and Yvonne Hester prayed for both their children before conception and while in the womb. Today as a Christian counselor, Harvey says he is thankful he and his wife had the foresight to bathe their daughters in prayers before birth.

Infants in the womb will remember what their mothers read to them, according to researchers at the University of North Carolina. Babies in their study responded after birth more vigorously to stories they had heard while in the womb than to others. I have heard of some expectant Christian mothers who read the Bible aloud and listen to Christian music for the sake of their *en utero* children.[3]

One father who prayed over two of his children before their birth said, "I'm convinced that we could change our entire nation by simply praying for our unborn and newly born children. It doesn't take special training, only love."

We as Christian mothers may feel we failed by complaining when we learned we had babies on the way. I did, too, at first with my third child. After all, we had one toddler and one infant and had just moved hundreds of miles from family and friends. But when it looked like I might lose the baby, I did everything I could to help her live—even staying in bed.

If we feel guilty, we can ask God to forgive us for not immediately accepting those "unwanted blessings." He knows we parents fail, and He's waiting patiently to forgive and restore us.

Today our "surprise baby" is studying for the mission field in the same state where she was born. God had a plan for her even then—twenty-two years ago. And He has one for each of our children.

Seventeen

Praying for Our Chronically Ill and Dying Children

"There is a time for everything…a time to be born and a time to die" (Eccles. 3:1,2).

There is such a fine line between helping a child fight to live and finally relinquishing him to death.

Sandy Prather has chosen to help her thirteen-year-old daughter Leah fight to live. The reason? She had a clear word from God to do so.

When Leah's headaches turned into the dreaded disease known as demyelinating encephalitis, Sandy rejected the doctor's report that her child had a slim chance of recovering. Even at this writing, Leah isn't out of danger, but she's fighting to live.

"Even when she was unconscious, unable to communicate, completely dependent on tube-feedings to keep her alive, I refused to believe the doctors' reports. Doctors told me what they knew in the natural, but in my heart I had God's word," Sandy told me.

"What word was that?" I asked.

"God showed me that although Satan comes to kill, steal, and destroy, he was not going to have my child. I read in Proverbs 6:31 that when a thief is found, he must repay sevenfold. I have determined to battle against the devil and see God snatch my daughter from his claws and returned to health in mind and body."

During the daytime, Sandy stays close to Leah's hospital bedside. She reads encouraging Bible passages aloud to her and tells her how much she loves her. She talks normally about what's going on in the family as though Leah understands every word. At night Sandy's husband keeps vigil by the bed.

"We never leave her alone. Otherwise, an unbelieving person might speak discouraging words to her," Sandy said. "I began feeding her small amounts of food until finally, though she couldn't communicate, she could take nourishment by mouth. I'm believing God to bring her to complete wholeness. All the medical people involved in her case are astonished by Leah's progress so far. I tell them God has assured my husband and me that she is coming out of this as a normal thirteen-year-old. We believe we will see it happen."

Sandy believes God has not only promised to heal Leah, but He also will bring it to pass.

"I believe all of our trials are designed to make us better, not bitter, to make us press towards God, not away from Him. Out of every dark experience comes a happy result. God's mercy and grace have been on me and my family through this," she added.

When Death is Imminent

We need God to give us keen discernment to know if He is going to heal a chronically ill person or if death is imminent. The apostle Peter once wrote, *"I know that I will soon put (my body) aside as our Lord Jesus Christ has made clear to me" (2 Pet. 1:14).*

In the United States particularly, we seldom talk to the terminally ill about death. If we know that death is near, do we do the patient an injustice when we talk lightly as if he is going back soon to his earthly home instead of to the heavenly one God has prepared for him?

In this day when cancer, AIDS, and other diseases are worldwide problems, we cannot piously pretend that every chronically or acutely ill person is going to be healed. Yes, of course we pray for healing, but we also try to lead our children to the Lord if they aren't saved. In God's economy, salvation takes priority over healing.

My prayer partner Fran Ewing is a nurse and physical therapist who has worked with many dying patients. What's more, her twenty-nine-year-old son Mark came close to the brink of death with advanced Hodgkin's disease three years ago. Fran knows firsthand what it is to face losing a child.

"We should remind our children that we are all going to face physical death sometime, unless we will be here when Jesus comes. I decided I had to prepare Mark for death or healing," she told me as she recalled her agonizing time of relinquishing Mark to God for His purposes to be worked out.

From her vast experience of dealing with the dying, Fran says as Christians we should (1) be sure the patient has accepted Jesus as his Savior and (2) stop pretending that the person is not dying. Instead, we should help him deal with the fear of dying common to all.

"We must be loving, gentle, and sensitive to the Holy Spirit in what we say," she told me.

"If we think he's near death, we want him to die without fear, with peace and assurance that 'to be absent from the body is to be present with the Lord,'" she explained.

She advises talking to such a child about his eternal being—that he is a spirit, he has a soul, and he lives in a body. The spirit within him will live on through eternity—with the Lord if he knows Him, in dark despair if he doesn't.

Fran gives an illustration which she found helpful in talking to her friend Dennie just before she slipped away. She suggests the mother of a young child could adapt it this way:

"Remember when we mailed Grandma a special gift last year? We selected it, bought it, then sealed it completely with tape for mailing. On the package, I wrote our return address, then Grandma's address. We took it to the post office, paid the postage, and gave it to the postmaster. He stamped it and put it aside to be shipped to Grandma.

"You are like that special package. Jesus bought you by giving His life for you. He sealed you with the Holy Spirit. Like the package waiting in the post office, you are waiting to be sent to our Father in heaven. We don't know when He'll send for you, but eventually an angel will deliver you to Him.

"We'll be separated for awhile, but Daddy and I will be along shortly, too, because Jesus also has bought us and is preparing us for sending to the Father. We know where we are going but we haven't been wrapped yet. Remember your friend who died? You'll see him and others you know. But the One you will know best is Jesus.

"Jesus left heaven to come down to earth to live, then to die for us so that He could go back to heaven and prepare a wonderful house for you and for me to come to.

"I'm going to sit here and hold your hand until Jesus sends for you, and then I'll place it in His hand."

Fran says we make a mistake when our children think this earth is all there is. We must teach them about heaven and that living on earth is only the tiniest slice of life.

Many times, mothers have not brought their little children to

Jesus, thinking they were too young or that the children had plenty of time later. It's never too late or too early. We should talk to our children about accepting Jesus even when they are small. Corrie ten Boom's mother helped her accept Jesus when she was five, and Corrie always remembered the exact moment.

We may be led to ask our dying children questions concerning forgiveness: "Is there anybody who's hurt you or that you are mad at? Let's pray and ask the Lord Jesus to forgive you." Fran says this often is an important first step to take when preparing a child for death.

She also emphasizes that mothers should read aloud scriptures which assure their children that there is no pain or sorrow where they are going and that they will have a far better life in heaven than they did on earth.

Paul left us encouragement in Romans 14:8: *"If we live, we live to the Lord; and if we die, we die to the Lord. So, whether we live or die, we belong to the Lord."*

That verse has a special meaning to me because that was my Mom's favorite as I helped her through thirteen months of agony before her death. I nursed her in the daytime and at night slept on a cot beside her bed. Besides talking a lot about our Savior, our favorite topics to discuss were healing, health, and heaven. I'll never forget those times spent searching the Scriptures for what God had to say on these subjects. Nor can I wipe away the memories of her final days when I read the Word aloud to her every morning. Although she couldn't respond, I knew in my spirit she was being comforted. Once she roused from her coma to shout three times, "Hallelujah! Hallelujah! Hallelujah!" These were her last words, although she lingered three more weeks. I was in her bedroom praying the Lord's Prayer when she died, an experience I'll forever cherish.

Here are some helpful scriptures to share with a loved one facing the end of his life on earth:

"Even though I walk through the valley of the shadow of death, I will fear no evil, for you are with me" (Ps. 23:4).

"So do not fear, for I am with you; do not be dismayed, for I am your God. I will strengthen you and help you; I will uphold you with my righteous right hand" (Isa. 41:10).

"And surely I will be with you always, to the very end of the age" (Matt. 28:20).

"If I rise on the wings of the dawn, if I settle on the far side of the sea, even there your hand will guide me, your right hand will hold me fast" (Ps. 139:9,10).

"Do not let your hearts be troubled. Trust in God; trust also in me. In my Father's house are many rooms; if it were not so, I would have told you. I am going there to prepare a place for you. And if I go and prepare a place for you, I will come back and take you to be with me that you also may be where I am. You know the way to the place where I am going" (John 14:1-3).

"And this is what he promised us—even eternal life" (1 John 2:25).

"See that you do not look down on one of these little ones. For I tell you that their angels in heaven always see the face of my Father in heaven" (Matt. 18:10).

"After the Lord Jesus had spoken to them, he was taken up into heaven and he sat at the right hand of God" (Mark 16:19).

Eighteen

Praying for Our Grandchildren

Paul wrote to Timothy: *"I have been reminded of your sincere faith, which first lived in your grandmother Lois and in your mother Eunice and, I am persuaded, now lives in you also"* (2 Tim. 1:5).

In our mobile society with the fabric of marriage being destroyed, grandparents have a deepening responsibility for their grandchildren. Many help raise their grandchildren while the parents work or may have full responsibility for them. Because of these possibilities, grandparents often directly influence the lives of those grandchildren—positively or negatively. What kind of influence will it be?

My own mom was not only my prime prayer warrior but she also was a great intercessor for her grandchildren.

Ten years before she died, she had a spiritual renewal—a powerful infilling of the Holy Spirit accompanied by a flowing prayer language.

She had been a good mother. She single-handedly raised and educated four children. I was twelve years old and the eldest when she was left alone. Mom earned our living running a boarding house in the shadow of the state capitol. Some forty boarders shared the house; another three hundred or more ate each day in her large dining room. College kids, construction workers, and state legislators came for family style meals, all they could eat for under a dollar.

Although mother had always attended church on Sundays, she developed a great love for Jesus and a burden to pray after she received the baptism in the Holy Spirit when she was sixty-two. By then she had ten grandchildren from crib to junior high age.

Whenever you'd ask Mother, "What's your greatest joy?" she'd wave both hands toward heaven and say, "To praise the Lord and to intercede for my ten grandchildren represented by these ten fingers."

When they were lonely, depressed, or in need of prayer, my children often called her from college with requests such as, "Mother Jewett, I've got such a hard test Friday, and I'm uptight about it. I need you to pray."

Mom would bombard heaven on behalf of that grandchild.

Mom seemed to have spiritual insights about our children that my husband and I didn't always have. She felt free to tell us when she thought we should "put feet" under our prayers.

Once after talking to one of our children who admitted to having difficulty in making his bankbook balance, Mother told my husband, "You need to get to that Florida State campus and see your two kids—if for nothing more than to encourage them with your presence. You need to praise them and praise God for their good qualities and stop looking at their faults."

LeRoy couldn't get off work to go, so at 5 a.m. the next day, I headed for Tallahassee with his blessing and some money for that college senior from his grandmother to balance his bankbook. Just before Keith graduated, she died. After commencement ceremonies as four of us stood outside, he clutched his diploma and looked up toward the sky. "I miss Mother Jewett so much. I wish she could have been here today. She helped me earn this with her prayers."

"She knew you'd succeed; she believed in you," I comforted him, wiping tears from my eyes.

I have no idea of the number of hours Mom prayed for my children—only God knows. She was both grandmother and granddaddy to them.

While caring for mother as she was dying of cancer, I'd read scriptures aloud during long nights in her home and she'd give me her input. Once when reading Proverbs 13:22, *"A good man leaves an inheritance for his children's children,"* she told me, "I want to leave them a spiritual inheritance."

"You've done that," I assured her.

When I read, *"Children's children are a crown to the aged,"* from Proverbs 17:6, she managed to say, "My grandchildren are truly my crown right now."

Two of my children made frequent trips from college to see Mother the last weeks of her life; they sat by her bed as she endured the final stages of the disease. It was their turn to pray for her.

"Why does she suffer so?" Keith agonized, smashing his fist into his open palm and weeping one Easter afternoon two days before her death.

"Darling, I don't know. But the Bible says, *'If we endure, we will also reign with him' (2 Tim. 2:12).* God's still got a purpose for her on earth. I can tell you she still prays for others. I know her well."

I often compared my mother to young Timothy's grandmother Lois. The apostle Paul tells us that from childhood Timothy had *"known the holy Scriptures"* which made him wise for *"salvation through faith in Christ Jesus* (2 Tim. 3:15). Obviously he learned these from his grandmother Lois and his mother Eunice, because Paul earlier mentions their faith (2 Tim. 1:3).

We've all been touched by reading the beautiful story of Ruth who returned with her mother-in-law Naomi to Bethlehem. We identify with Ruth, but what about faithful Naomi? When Ruth married, Naomi had a new lease on life because she gained a precious grandson.

Naomi's friends said to her, *"May he become famous throughout Israel! He will renew your life and sustain you in your old age" (Ruth 4:14,15).*

Naomi took the child on her lap and cared for him. Don't you know she prayed often for that special little boy? And how special he was, for he was Obed, the father of Jesse and grandfather of King David.

One grandmother I know prays Scripture prayers aloud for her grandchildren daily. She told me she likes to paraphrase the Psalms, like this: "Guard my grandson Tom, in all his ways. Be his stronghold in time of trouble. Help him and deliver him from the wicked. Save him because he takes refuge in You" (37:39,40).

In 1820 a tiny baby girl, Frances Jane, became blind when given the wrong eye medication. Instead of becoming bitter as she grew older, she responded to the training of her faithful grandmother who helped her memorize much of the Bible. From the time she was young until she died at the age of eighty-six, there flowed from that granddaughter over three thousand hymns and gospel songs. We know the blind songwriter as Fanny Crosby and often sing the songs she left as a legacy—"Blessed Assurance," "All The Way My Savior Leads Me," "Rescue The Perishing," and hundreds of others.[1]

No, never underestimate the virtuous influence of a godly

grandmother.

I love to visit my former prayer partner Lib and watch as she sits in the swing under her shady elm and sings about Jesus to one of her three grandchildren, Joshua, Rachel, or Kira. From her they've learned to lift their little arms and say, "Praise You, Jesus." From her, they've learned goodnight prayers.

"This is the best stage of my life—my greatest privilege— helping with these three grandchildren," she told me last week when I drove the four hundred and fifty miles to see her and the newest one.

As her husband Gene tucked two-year-old Joshua into bed for a nap, he prayed for him as he does whenever they baby-sit. Watching this, I was reminded of Jacob calling Joseph's two sons to him and blessing them just before he died. Grandparents in biblical days had much influence in their grandchildren's lives. I'm sure the righteous ones constantly prayed for their grandchildren.

If we have grandchildren, we have the rare privilege of nurturing them in the love of the Lord. God can make us positive influences in their lives as we pray for them.

Nineteen

Praying Without Guilt

"If you live in Me—abide vitally united to Me—and My words remain in you and continue to live in your hearts, ask whatever you will and it shall be done for you" (John 15:7 TAB).

So often we feel that what we do for our children is too little and too late. We are then guilt-ridden with "if only." If only we had prayed sooner, taught earlier, loved more, communicated better. If only....

Can we trust God who does everything in the right way and the right time? Can we ask God's forgiveness (and sometimes our own kids' as well) for our failures as parents, then trust Him? If we want to be "anxious for nothing," we have to trust.

I've had to ask my children to forgive me many times, and I expect I'll have to ask again. Actually, when we sow forgiveness, we reap forgiveness. Most importantly, when we have an attitude of forgiveness, we keep open our own communication lines with God.

Every child of His, every born-again believer, has promises from the heavenly Father on which to base his life. When we read through the Bible, we find many promises applying to our individual family's difficulty. Only God knows when our particular situation is fully ripe for His answer. While we wait with faith and patience to inherit those promises, we can be reassured by these verses as faith-builders:

"Now faith is being sure of what we hope for and certain of what we do not see" (Heb. 11:1).

"Be still before the Lord and wait patiently for him" (Ps. 37:7).

"Let us hold unswervingly to the hope we profess, for he who promised is faithful" (Heb. 10:23).

"I am the Lord, the God of all mankind. Is anything too hard for me?" (Jer. 32:26).

Yes, what a privilege is ours when we go to the very throne room of God in prayer on behalf of our children and grandchildren.

When we do this regularly, we can pray without guilt.

Twenty

Leaving a Legacy of Prayer

"In bitterness of soul Hannah wept much and prayed to the Lord. And she made a vow, saying, 'O Lord Almighty, if you will only look upon your servant's misery and remember me, and not forget your servant but give her a son, then I will give him to the Lord for all the days of his life'" (1 Sam. 1:10,11).

If we want our children to pray, they must hear us pray. The greatest demonstration of God's power to our children is knowing that we parents get answers to our prayers. This happens when they've heard us pray and seen the results.

Let's study Hannah's first prayer for a moment, the one she breathed in silence in the temple as the priest Eli watched. Her lips moved but her voice was not heard. Yet what she said to God was recorded, no doubt because she later told Samuel what she had prayed.

Hers is the first recorded prayer of a woman in the Old Testament. Her request was specific, "Give me a son." She asked God to change her circumstances since she was barren. Three times she humbled herself, calling herself a "servant." Unselfish in her petition, she vowed to give up her child to God.

Hannah was honest before God. She meant business with Him. She even risked being misunderstood by the priest who thought she was drunk.

But through Eli, God told her that her request would be granted.In the course of time, Hanna conceived and gave birth to a son whom she named Samuel, saying, *"Because I asked the Lord for him" (1 Sam. 1:20).*

By the time of her second prayer, Hannah has matured in her prayer life. She begins with her feelings but ends by praising God for His power, His righteousness. Finally, she prophesies that God will give strength to His king—in a land which had never had a king before. Eventually, her firstborn son Samuel would anoint Israel's first king.

Sometimes we forget that Hannah had three sons and two daughters born after Samuel. How God heard her prayers.

Samuel's name came from two words, *eli,* which is Hebrew for God, and *samu* meaning, "I ask." He knew from earliest childhood his mother's prayers were answered. Every time she called his name, she was saying, "I asked God."

What a legacy she left him.

And what a legacy we can leave our children, a legacy of prayer.

If we've ever meditated on Mary's prayer before the birth of Jesus, we can't help but notice that it resembles Hannah's magnificent praise-prayer. How precious it is that we have these women's prayers recorded as patterns for us to pray out loud. They also encourage us to write out our prayers to leave for our children and their children after them.

Author Catherine Marshall kept a journal most of her life and often recorded her prayers. In her books *Adventures in Prayer, Something More,* and *Beyond Ourselves,* she gives wonderful examples of prayers answered on behalf of her children—from their returning to the Lord after rebellious periods to finding just the right spouses.

Charles Spurgeon once wrote, "My own conversion is a result of prayer. Long, affectionate, earnest and importunate—my parents prayed for.me. God heard their cries, and here I am to preach the Gospel." How did he know? He heard them praying.

The Scriptures clearly admonish Christian parents to instruct their children in the ways of God. We are told to teach His commandments to our children, to talk about them when we sit at home and when we walk along the road, when we lie down and when we get up (Deut. 6:7). I believe this includes praying aloud for them, letting them hear us when we lie down at night or arise in the morning.

Then, too, there's the importance of written prayers. I've made it a practice to write out prayers for my children to include in letters I'm sending them. Sometimes I type a prayer or a scripture verse on a three-by-five-inch card so they can post it on their mirrors for daily reminders to pray along with me.

I get excited every time I read the verse that says God keeps *"his covenant of love to a thousand generations of those who love him and keep his commands" (Deut. 7:9).* What an inheritance that is!

Let us pass on to our children the greatest inheritance possible—our personal prayer lives that they can model after.

In the past year I've watched my two daughters almost outdistance me in their prayer lives. I pray they will continue to grow and share with me new ways the Holy Spirit is teaching them to pray, so that when they have children, together we can teach them to pray.

This is my prayer for all of us and our children.

NOTES

Chapter 11
1. Ruth Graham, "A Mother's View," *Christian Life*, Nov. 1984, p. 52.
2. Charles Colson, *Loving God* (Grand Rapids: Zondervan, 1984), pp. 45-53.

Chapter 16
1. Thomas R. Verny, *The Secret Life of the Unborn Child* (New York: Summit Books, 1981), pp. 19, 20.
2. Francis MacNutt, "Prayers for the Unborn," *Charisma*, Nov. 1983, p. 28.

Chapter 18
1. Bernard Ruffin, *Fanny Crosby* (New York: Pilgrim Press, 1976), pp. 20, 30, 255.

Inquiries regarding speaking availability and other correspondence may be directed to Quin Sherrer at the following address:

P.O. Box 25433
Colorado Springs, CO 80936